Louder Than Rock

by

Caleb Quaye
with Dale A. Berryhill

Published by New World Music
MinistriesPublishing LLC

Revised Edition ©2022

[Note: Scripture references are from the New King James version of the Bible.]

Table of Contents:

Chapter 1. The Peak

Chapter 2. Beginnings

Chapter 3. Denmark Street

Chapter 4. The Great Purge

Chapter 5. The Butterfly Emerges

Chapter 6. Hookfoot

Chapter 7. Back With Elton

Chapter 8. Hotel Damascus

Chapter 9. A New Life

Chapter 10. Reunited

Chapter 11. On The Road Again

Chapter 12. The Glamorous Life

Chapter 13. The Rebellious Heart

Acknowledgements

First of all, I thank my Lord and Savior Jesus Christ for coming to my rescue in 1982, and giving me a life I could not have achieved on my own. And thanks to Chester and Roz Thompson for a conversation over an African stew that led to a transformed life.

Thanks to my wife, Lydia, and my daughters, Lucy, Melissa, and Stephanie, for the endless supply of love, friendship, and support.

Thanks to Tom Stanton, founder and editor (until 2001) of the excellent *East End Lights* magazine, a publication for Elton John fans that always surpassed the status of mere "fanzine." My series of interviews with John Higgins, along with my subsequent appearance at the magazine's 1996 Elton Expo, led to the writing and publication of this book by introducing me to my co-author, *East End Lights* writer Dale A. Berryhill.

Much appreciation to my old friend and bandmate Roger Pope for submitting himself to extensive interviews in an attempt to help me remember those hazy days of the past. Between the two of us, I think we recovered most of our memories!

I also hold fond remembrances of producer extraordinaire Gus Dudgeon, who filled in many blanks on the technical side of our recordings that I never would have known otherwise. The sudden loss of Gus and his wife Sheila in an automobile accident during the writing of this book, along with the more recent loss of Roger Pope, are poignant reminders of the temporary nature of life in this realm. Our prayers remain with their friends and families.

Assistance in researching several questions was generously volunteered by Jim McKay, founder and moderator of The 22nd Row, the first major Internet discussion group for Elton John fans, and Alan McCormick, owner and operator of the Elton John direct mail service Wrap It Up until his untimely death in 2016.

Thanks also to the following for reviewing the manuscript and making helpful suggestions for improvement: Jim McKay, John Phillips, Andrew Lauder, René Berryhill, Darren Nathen. Assistance on the revised version was graciously provided by

Rhiannon Connor.

Finally, thanks to Vision Publishing's Stanley O. Williford for seeing the possibilities of this book getting out when it seemed that all the doors had closed.

Introduction

From the 1960s to the 1980s, I played and recorded with some of the top names in rock & roll —Paul McCartney, Mick Jagger, Pete Townshend, Lou Reed, Hall & Oates, and, most notably, Elton John. Today, as a Christian minister, I can honestly say that the glamour of those days and the celebrity of those names mean absolutely nothing to me. I have no desire to exploit my connection to these famous musicians, especially my close association with Elton John, an association that began in friendship and, I hope, remains grounded in friendship today.

Why, then, am I writing this book? The answer is that I'm the father of three children, and

I'm aware from personal experience of the influence that music wields upon young people. I don't really know why, but music is like a drug to teenagers. Music is also the language of culture, and today the music of our culture far too often focuses on despair, pain, and cynicism, when it could be offering hope, promoting optimism, praising virtue, and celebrating life. I believe this to be nothing less than a misuse of a blessing bestowed upon us by God.

You see, I believe that God gave us the gift of music. When we're in a right relationship with Him, we can enjoy and rejoice in the positive aspects of this gift. I'm not saying that all music must be specifically Christian music, or even religious in a general sense. You don't have to be a religious person to see that music is one of the most beautiful gifts of life, yet our music industry so often uses it as a vehicle for portraying the most negative aspects of life. I despair at seeing so many young people influenced by music that is calculated to make them angry, to separate them from their parents, and to encourage them to experiment with harmful behavior.

Like the movie and television industries, the music industry exploits the worst in people. Much of today's entertainment plays off of people's worst tendencies and temptations—violence, sex, cynicism, skepticism, disrespect for authority, and escapism. In doing so, the entertainment industry takes God's greatest gifts and perverts them. In Hollywood, our most beautiful women are reduced

9

to mere objects. Human sexuality, designed by God to be an important part of a sacred bonding between two married people, is reduced to a spectator sport of increasing decadence and detachment. The precious gift of laughter is reduced to a mechanized rote response to any rude or suggestive statement. Even basic human communication is reduced to outbursts of anger and profanity.

All this is skillfully packaged and promoted as being reflective of our society, and perhaps it is. But as a musician and a producer, I can tell you that most of the people who are writing our songs and screenplays, recording our music, and filming our movies can hardly keep their own lives afloat, much less tell others how to live. I have personally seen so many gifted people mess up and even lose their lives in the quest for fame, fortune, acceptance, or whatever it was they thought they were going to get out of show business. How sad that these are our children's role models, the people providing the background music to our children's lives.

You see, the entertainment industry is a deceiver. It's a hypocritical industry—one that talks about feminism while exploiting women, talks about civil rights while exploiting and encouraging black anger, promotes liberal do-goodism while wallowing in hedonism and greed, claims to speak for the average person while its members live in mansions and ride around in limousines, and justifies itself on the grounds that it is reflective of reality while promoting escapist behavior such as drug use.

If you don't believe the entertainment industry is hypocritical, ask yourself this: Why does it strongly deny that profanity and sexual images will affect young people, then strongly protest that there aren't enough positive role models on television for women and minorities? The industry knows full well that the images and sounds they produce really do have an impact on people's attitudes and behavior. If that weren't the case, they wouldn't be able to charge advertisers millions of dollars to promote their products!

Today's entertainment industry not only cannot offer a cure for the pain and despair of the times, it is actively involved in exploiting, promoting, and deepening that pain and despair. Why? Because it makes money that way. The industry has a vested interest in keeping young people unhappy and angst-ridden, because it can sell products to them that tap into that unhappiness and angst. Teenagers are an easy target because they're still trying to find their own identity, their goals in life, their values. They're frustrated, confused, and impatient, just as we all were at that age. What they need is love, encouragement, guidance, and support in their decisions. What they get from the entertainment industry is a vehicle for wallowing more and more deeply in their confusion. If America's teenagers came out of their haze, dropped the drugs, got jobs, and focused on their grades, a large percentage of the market for music, movies, and video games would disappear.

As an example, think what would happen to

the rap music industry if we woke up tomorrow and racism had disappeared. What if people stopped noticing skin color and African-Americans finally realized Martin Luther King, Jr.'s dream of fully entering the mainstream of society? What if young blacks in the inner cities stopped being angry, shunned the "gangsta" mentality, and started focusing on improving their own educations and succeeding in their careers? Why, the music industry would lose billions! The multi-billion dollar rap music industry is based entirely on keeping the African-American culture distinct from society as a whole and on encouraging young African-Americans to despise white America. The fact that this industry began by tapping into some real existing anger doesn't legitimize its motives or excuse the role it plays.

Yes, the entertainment industry is a deceiver, and the people in it are not qualified to serve as anyone's role models. I know—I was one of those people, and my story is a living example of how the industry fails to keep its promises. It is also a warning about the pitfalls of fame, blind ambition, and worldly success.

Still, my purpose in telling this story is not to sensationalize the negative aspects of the entertainment industry, but to point to something more positive. When I was hobnobbing with some of the biggest stars popular music has ever produced, I thought I had what matters in life. If I had stopped to think about it, I would have dismissed the idea of religious faith as something unreal. Today, I see that it was the fame and the success that were unreal and transient, while it is my religious faith that is meaningful and lasting.

What the music business has, I don't need, but what I have in my heart, the music business needs. What I have in my heart is needed by all the famous people I've worked with through the years. What I have in my heart is needed by the young people who turn to rock music in a vain search for an antidote to the pain and despair they feel. What I have in my heart is a living relationship with Jesus Christ.

My only prayer is that this book will help at least one hurting, despairing person to look the other way—to look up instead of down—and to open his or her heart to Jesus, who ever lives, and who makes intercession for us with God the Father (or who, as the hit song from the '60s says, is "gonna set me up with the Spirit in the Sky").

No matter how badly you've been mistreated and betrayed by people—even by your own family—life can still be a joyous thing. But you won't find joy by turning to those who peddle despair. You will find joy by turning to the One who offers you a solution to your despair.

Are you willing to let your despair go? Are you willing to admit that you're not in control? Are you tired of playing the game of holding people at arm's length while complaining that no one cares? Are you tired of feeling sorry for yourself? Are you ready to get on with your life? Well, after all the success and money and fame I enjoyed for almost two decades, I ended up right where you are. Let

me tell you what I did about it.

Chapter One

The Peak

What I remember most about that day was how incredibly sharp and clear it all was. It was as if I could see every individual fan in the stadium from the stage—every colorful shirt, every bouncing face, every waving arm. Roger hit his drumsticks together to set the tempo, Davey and I slashed at our guitar strings, and the crowd roared.

The roar of 50,000 people is hard to describe when it's directed at you, and as experienced a rock musician as I was, it made me catch my breath a bit. I didn't think that roar could get any louder, but it rose to new levels when Elton John walked out on stage wearing a sequined replica of a Los Angeles

Dodgers baseball uniform. To this sell-out crowd at Dodger Stadium, it couldn't get any better than this. Elton had the audience in the palm of his hand from the beginning, but when he picked up a baseball bat and began swatting tennis balls far out into the crowd, he owned the heart and soul of every kid there.

It seemed as if all of Los Angeles had turned out for these shows. And it was quite a production. Elton had enlisted the services of the Rev. James Cleveland and his gospel choir, who would also perform on his next album, *Blue Moves*. Tennis legend Billie Jean King came on stage to help sing backup vocals to "Philadelphia Freedom," the song Elton had written in her honor. When Elton introduced the members of the band, our names appeared on the stadium's electronic scoreboards. The concert was being filmed for BBC television back home. Needless to say, the entire experience gave us an overwhelming sense of having "arrived."

Playing rock & roll to crowds of 50,000 or more is commonplace today, but in 1975 it was a new phenomenon. Furthermore, this was a history-making concert. We were the first band to play Dodger Stadium since The Beatles ten years before, and we were playing to sell-out crowds two days in a row. In fact, we were breaking attendance records in venues across America. The following year, we would become the first band to play seven straight sell-out concerts in Madison Square Garden.

Since then, of course, Elton has gone on to play to much larger audiences, as have other bands.

But those concerts in Dodger Stadium were the biggest thing that had happened to any rock & roll act up to that point. Not only that, but they occurred at the end of a streak of six consecutive number-one studio albums, second only to The Beatles at that time. Despite all of his incredible success since then, these concerts were, in a very real sense, the peak of Elton John's career.

Elton was aware of what this weekend meant. He had spent tens of thousands of dollars to fly an entire planeload of family, friends, and record company staff members from England over to L.A. He rented the former home of Greta Garbo in Beverly Hills to stay in. We all celebrated in style, knowing that if it all ended next week, we would forever remain a part of rock & roll history.

And it wasn't just Elton's triumph; it was mine as well. I was Elton's oldest friend in the music industry, having met him when we were both teenage errand boys running around Denmark Street, Britain's Tin Pan Alley. I had produced his earliest demos, helped convince the record company to give him his first contract, and played guitar on his early albums. Apart from Elton, I had produced and played with some of the biggest names in rock & roll. I had played on Lou Reed's first solo album, Pete Townshend's first solo album, and the soundtrack to The Who's *Tommy*. I had produced demos for groups like The Hollies, Gerry & The Pacemakers, and Billy J. Kramer & The Dakotas. My own band, Hookfoot, had released four albums, played before huge audiences at rock festivals, and toured with groups like Humble Pie.

Remember The Troggs' 1968 Top Ten hit "Love is All Around?" You can hear my guitar on that one. Remember Nilsson's 1972 odd little Top Ten hit "Coconut"? That's me again.

For almost a decade, I had been recognized among those in the music industry as one of the top guitarists around. But without question, this weekend in L.A. was the height, the peak, as high as one could go. As I was to find out all too soon, there was nowhere to go from here but down.

Even during that weekend, there was trouble in paradise. Two days before the concert, with his mother and all his friends sitting around the pool at the house he was renting, Elton came out of his room, announced that he had taken more than seventy Valium tablets, and jumped into the pool. Now, Elton was always good at getting attention (as anyone who has ever seen one of his shows knows) and an earlier suicide attempt was already firmly established in Elton folklore, having been part of the inspiration for the song "Someone Saved My Life Tonight." But in this case, we really feared for a little while that he wouldn't make it. The medics pumped his stomach, but he lingered in semi-consciousness throughout the night. The management and the members of the band even had a meeting to begin facing the very real possibility that this tour—and this brilliant career—might be abruptly ended.

During those first hours when we were most shocked and fearful, I was standing by the pool with

Elton's mother and grandmother, who had known me since I was a young teenager. His mother, as she had done so many times before, turned to me with her begging eyes and said, "Oh, Caleb, can't you talk to him?" But this time I couldn't look into those eyes. I was one of the ones who had helped turn Elton on to drugs.

Finally, the next day, we got word that he was okay, and that the concerts would go on as scheduled. I honestly believe that the performances at those concerts were so superb because we were all releasing this incredible mixture of emotions—relief, fear, happiness, sadness, frustration, anger. The concerts were cathartic after all that had come before. To this day I remember those concerts with a strange mixture of emotions.

You see, Elton wasn't the only one having trouble enjoying his success. People kept telling me, "Hey, congratulations, Caleb. You've really made it." But at night, after the rush of the show and after all the celebrating and the drugs and the groupies, I would go back to my hotel room alone. In the mirror I would see this sweating mess that I had become. And as I had done so many times before, I would say to myself, "There's got to be more to it than this."

Little did I know that my life was about to take a sharp downward spiral from this peak. Little did anyone know that the same thing would happen to Elton. Elton and I were about to go our separate ways, but we were to follow eerily similar paths. Both of us would hit low points in our careers, followed by a long, hard period of struggling with —and coming to terms with—the personal demons we had so long tried to ignore. Both of us would be forced to acknowledge our own weaknesses and to declare our reliance on a "higher power" to help us overcome our many addictions. In the end, we would both emerge clean and sober.

But there is one significant difference between my triumph and Elton's: My higher power has a name.

Chapter Two

Beginnings

I come from four generations of musicians. My great grandfather, Henry Quaye, was an *asopho* in the Gha tribe in Ghana in West Africa. The *asopho* were musician-warrior-priests who would go in front of the tribe playing the drums during battle or on a hunting expedition. When the tribe was converted to Christianity by Methodist missionaries, he became the minister of the Jamestown Methodist Cathedral in Accra, Ghana. (Today a minister in the church in Ghana is still called *asopho*, which now translates to "reverend.")

My paternal grandfather—who was named Caleb Quaye—played the organ in my great-grandfather's church. He was a piano player of amazing ability. As a young man, he would entertain the tourists on the ships docked at the port at Accra, where he got to know several sailors who happened to be jazz musicians. He was often told that, with his musical abilities, he could make a great living in England. He started saving money for his fare, and one day he snuck out so his parents couldn't stop him and sailed away on one of the ships. As in the story of Dick Whittington, who left his home in the English countryside to find his fortune in London, my grandfather left Accra to find out if the streets of London were paved with gold. In London he found some of the friends he had met on the ships, and they helped him start his musical career. He established a jazz band called The Five

Musical Dragons that soon became famous throughout England and Europe.

Caleb married an English showgirl, and in 1920 my father—Augustus Kwamlah Quaye—was born. But when my father was just one year old, my grandfather was killed in a train wreck on the way to a gig in Wolverhampton. He was only twenty-six years old, and his death led my grandmother to become an alcoholic. She later married a man who turned out to be an abusive stepfather. That's the environment my father grew up in.

Despite all these setbacks, my father also grew up to be a famous musician in Europe—a jazz pianist who played under the name of Cab Kaye. He also grew up to become a drug addict and an alcoholic. My father's life was living proof that fame does not make you happy, or healthy, or a good person. Unfortunately, that was a lesson I would have to learn all over on my own.

In 1939, he married my mother, Theresa Austin, and I was born on October 9, 1948. I grew up in a small town in greater London called Finchley. I attended public schools and a couple of Anglican church schools. My sister Terri is eight years older than me, and my sister Tanya is four years younger. We were all musicians; we all sang. I started playing the piano when I was four years old, and I turned out to be somewhat of a child prodigy. My Dad had taught me how to play the "boogie-woogie" on the piano and I began to win music contests at a young age. Several times I appeared in the newspaper for this, and they always wanted my dad in the shot with me. They never failed to mention that I was the son of the famous Cab Kaye and that I was clearly following in my father's footsteps. Sadly, that turned out to be true in more ways than one.

Whenever my father was in town, which wasn't often, he would have his band over on Sunday afternoons to rehearse. My mother and grandmother would cook the Sunday dinner, and after we were through, my father and these musicians would go into the front room (what Americans call the living room) and they would jam. His band had sax players and trumpet players, so they could really put out some noise, especially in that enclosed space. We'd sit in the dining room and listen to them play, and after a while, I would sneak into the front room and sit on the floor to watch them. It wasn't hard to sneak in without being seen, because the air in the room would be filled with smoke as thick as pea soup. Every member of the band, including my father, would be smoking marijuana.

    These jam sessions didn't happen all that often, because the band was always on the road. The truth is that I never really knew my father when I was growing up. One time he was on tour for two years and didn't come home the entire time. My mom had to work two or three jobs to support the family. I don't know how she did it. She kept us all going. There was always food on the table, but I know it was very tough on her.

When my father was in town, I didn't look forward to going home because there were always arguments, fighting, and swearing. He would often get drunk and go on a rampage of physical and verbal abuse. One day, when I was about four years old, I watched my father, in a drunken rage, pick up my maternal grandmother, lift her over his head, and throw her down the stairs. Another time he beat my older sister so badly that he nearly blinded her in one eye. She had to leave home and live with one of her friends, and she had to have police protection from my father.

One day when I was a little older—between seven and nine years old—my father came home from drinking with his friends in the park. He was in such a drunken rage that the veins were sticking out on his neck. He ordered our whole family to get into the car. I didn't know where we were going or what was going on, but I just knew that something terrible was going to happen. My mother scurried around telling us to do as he said and not to upset him. So we all got into the car and my father proceeded to drive around. The roads in that area are typical English roads—twisting and narrow. My father drove as fast as he could and went through every single red light without even slowing down. He was trying to kill the whole family. That's what he wanted to do. I didn't understand the reasons because I was too young, but I knew that that's what he wanted to do. We sat in the back absolutely petrified. I'll never forget it. I know that God prevented us from dying that day.

Later, when I was about sixteen or seventeen years old, my mother had a nervous breakdown. She had to be institutionalized for eighteen months. My mother is a very private person, the kind who doesn't share her feelings with others. Like most abused women, she didn't have many friends. She was a very loving person, but she would keep things bottled up inside, and finally one day her mind couldn't take it anymore, and she snapped. I remember walking into her bedroom one day and saying, "How are you feeling today, Mum?" She looked at me and said, "Who are you?" She later recovered completely, but I'll never forget the sick feeling in my heart when my own mother didn't recognize me.

Still, I could understand what had happened

because, like her, I didn't know what to do with all the bad feelings and the sorrow and the anguish that came from living in that household. The only place I could find rest was in music. In my early childhood, I loved sitting there on the floor of the front room on those Sunday afternoons, watching my father hunched over the keyboard or playing the guitar. I was this wide-eyed kid listening to all this music in my house, and I thought it was great. That's why I started playing piano and winning those contests—I wanted to be like my father. By the age of seven I was playing the drums. By the age of ten I wanted to learn to play the guitar, and that led to one of the most painful things that ever happened between my father and me.

    Just before my tenth birthday, he asked,

"Son, what do you want for your birthday?"

I said, "Dad, I would love a guitar," because I wanted to be like him. He replied, "Okay, son, I'll get you a guitar." But when my birthday came, he'd gotten me something else. He'd forgotten. On my eleventh birthday, exactly the same thing happened. Finally, on my twelfth birthday, he took me downtown to a pawn shop and bought me the cheapest guitar he could find. The strings were about half an inch off the board and it was really difficult to play, but I was so thrilled that he'd gotten me this guitar. I was excited because I thought this was something we could do together. I thought he would teach me how to play. We got home and went into the living room. He sat down at the piano, took the guitar from me, and started tuning it up. He showed me what the notes were on the piano. I was thinking, "Man, this is great. I'm about to get my first guitar lesson." But as soon as he finished tuning it up, he gave it back to me and said, "Here you are. You're on your own now." And he got up and left.

    I was stunned. "You're on your own." I was too young to understand just how deeply I was hurt, or what a profound sense of abandonment this created. Instead, I got angry. "Okay, fine," I said to myself. If he was going to leave me on my own, then I was going to show him that I could make it on my own. I decided on that day that I was going to become one of the best guitar players in the world. In the months to come, I would play that guitar until my fingers bled. I never took a single lesson—I just listened to records and picked out the notes, or made up tunes of my own. That's how I learned, and that's how I developed a personal style that later made me much in demand. It was all inspired by my father, although not in a good way.

About two weeks after buying me the guitar, he left for good. He went to Ghana, where his father was from. He went over there to lead a life in politics and music, and I didn't see him again for ten years. On the day he left, my sister and I looked at each other and said, "Thank goodness he's gone. We'll have some peace now."

My grades had been reasonably good up until that time, but after this they started to sink. Despite the problems that had always been going on at home, I had actually been a very happy kid. I was not a loner; I wasn't a depressed kid. I always had a lot of friends; I was always very sociable. I was athletic, so in school I participated in track and field, swimming, diving, soccer, and gymnastics. All in all, I had a great childhood. But after my father left us, music became my life, and everything else began to slip. I quit going out and playing football with the guys. My girlfriends would get fed up with me and say, "All you care about is playing your guitar." And I'd say, "Yep. Goodbye." That's how it was for me. After all, I knew my guitar would never hurt me or betray me or leave me. Besides, I had something to prove.

I became more and more determined to "make it" as a professional musician, despite my mother's attempts to persuade me otherwise. I'm sure it added to her grief to see me let everything else go. But that's the perverse way that Satan turns misery into more misery. Here I was, sacrificing everything to try to be like the very man who had hurt me the most. Here I was, trying to prove something to a man who didn't even care if I was alive. All I could hear was his statement, "You're on your own," ringing in my ears.

I've since learned that it's very common for children who are unloved to become ultra-independent. We tell ourselves that we don't need anyone as a defense mechanism against the pain of being abandoned by those we count on. Like so many others in that situation, I didn't care what anyone else thought. I never became a mean person, just an uncaring one. I erected barriers around my heart that no one could penetrate.

    My family didn't attend church during my childhood. My mother had joined the Catholic Church when she was young, but she had left it when she was nineteen. My father hated the church, his stated reason being the church's role in perpetuating racial intolerance. He told me about one time when he had attended a movie made by a black production company in America that told the biblical story with all the characters played by blacks. After the movie ended, the theater thought it necessary to have a white vicar come out and explain that, of course, God is not really black, and that this was merely "the colored version' of biblical events. My father, furious, stormed out.

    When I was ten, my father took me to St.

Mary's Church, an Episcopal church in Finchley built in the 12th century, and signed me up for the choir. He did this to help keep me out of trouble. I really enjoyed it, and before long I became the head choirboy. Our choir would even sing at St. Paul's Cathedral on special occasions. One of my fellow choir mates was Chris Squire, who was later the bass player for the rock group Yes. But while all this was going on, no one in my family attended church with me.

Soon after I turned fifteen, I began to notice that a lot of my friends in the church were being confirmed. Every time the church held a confirmation service, several of my friends would walk down the aisle and be blessed by the church. Afterward, they would proudly display their certificate of confirmation. I saw this as a sign of approval that I wanted for myself. I inquired and found out that you had to be baptized before you could be confirmed. Because the Church of England practices infant baptism, I didn't even know whether I had been baptized, so I asked my mother. She told me I had not.

"Why?" I asked.

"Because your father never had the time."

Well, that made me angry. I was embarrassed to learn that, after five years of service to the church, I didn't qualify to be confirmed in the church. I felt like a huge hypocrite, standing there and singing every Sunday morning, and even being recognized as the head choirboy, when in fact I wasn't really a part of the church.

That was it for me. I quit the church. Several months later, I quit school, as well.

Two years before, when I was fourteen, I had transferred to Hillside Secondary Modern. I was in a group of kids that were put into an experimental class. We were the musicians, the artists, the weirdos, the misfits—kids who weren't dumb enough to be kicked out of the school, but who didn't conform to traditional academic standards enough to succeed. You had A students, B students, and we were XG—Experimental General. I remember one day, when I had been acting up in class, the teacher dragged me to the front of the room and announced that I would never amount to anything. That was the last class I attended in school. At the Easter break, I dropped out.

I came home on a Friday in the spring of 1964 and showed my mother my report card, which was terrible, and told her I wasn't going back to school. She said, "All right, I want you to get on the tube [subway] tomorrow and go out looking for a job, and don't bother coming home until you've got one." Well, I knew what kind of job I wanted. My father was a famous musician, and I was committed to becoming a famous musician myself.

Naturally, I was heavily into the popular music of the day, and you have to understand what that meant to a teenage boy in London in 1964. It meant The Beatles, The Rolling Stones, and all the other British groups who were remaking rock & roll and, in the process, becoming the biggest stars on the planet. And it was all happening right there in my hometown.

The first wave of rock & roll had come from America—our heroes were Elvis Presley, Jerry Lee Lewis, Little Richard, Chuck Berry, Buddy Holly, and Gene Vincent. But by the late '50s, scandals had put the careers of Lewis and Berry on hold, and Elvis had gone off to join the U.S. Army. Alan Freed, the American deejay who had done the most to promote rock music, had been fired after a payola scandal. The music industry in America, recognizing a cash cow in rock music but afraid of the controversy, had turned to squeaky-clean, pre-fabricated pop idols. The influence of black music on rock was kept carefully under wraps, and the music was polished to middle-of-the-road "bubblegum" that could only be called rock & roll because it happened to have a back beat.

But on the other side of the Atlantic, scruffy English schoolboys like me were still turned on to real rock & roll, as well as to the jazz, blues, and rhythm & blues that had spawned it. Ironically, it was British groups like The Beatles, The Stones, and The Who that were reviving this American art form. The second wave of rock & roll was distinctly British, so much so that Americans dubbed it the "British Invasion." Needless to say, I wanted to be a part of it.

So the morning after I told my mum I was dropping out of school, I jumped on the tube train and went downtown to Soho, the headquarters of the music industry. I walked the streets of London on a Saturday looking for a job in the music business. Surprisingly, I got one that day. I was to start on Monday as an office boy in a place called Paxton's, a wholesale music distributor.

Boy, was I pleased! I'd gotten a job in the music business! I would make a whopping five pounds a week (and, no, five pounds wasn't much even back then). But to me, it was wonderful, for it symbolized freedom at last.

As it turned out, I was half right. Like so many people before and since, I found that the music industry freed me and enslaved me at the same time. The freedom would be heaven; the enslavement would be hell. But the prison it built around me would be such a gilded cage that it would take me years to realize what it was doing to me.

Chapter Three

Denmark Street

Soho in 1964 was a bustling place, an exciting place, especially in the eyes of a 15-year-old boy. Soho is an area in downtown London measuring one square mile, and it was and is the center of the city's nightlife. It's where all the nightclubs are, which in those days meant famous spots like The Marquee Club and The Flamingo. Chinatown is in Soho, so there were lots of great Chinese restaurants, as well as Indian and other types of restaurants. It was also London's red light district, with lots of strip joints, prostitution, and drug dealing.

During the day, Soho served as the center of

England's entertainment industry. Denmark Street —a short street only a few hundred yards long— was Britain's Tin Pan Alley, the center of its music industry. Every building in that street was a music publishing company or a recording studio, and toward one end of the street was a restaurant called The Gioconda where all the music people would go. The food was plain English fare—sausage, beans, chips, and a cup of tea—and on the walls were photographs of all the popular musical artists who had eaten there. In the mid-'60s, that meant The Beatles, The Kinks, The Who, The Stones and many other lesser names. Right next to the Gioconda was Regent Sound Studios, a basement studio with a three-track recorder where The Stones had recorded their first efforts, "Come On" and "I Wanna Be

Your Man."

Musicians from all parts of the country came to Denmark Street to pitch their demos, to record their next albums, to soak up the creative energy. Donovan was down there, The Hollies, The Small Faces, The Ivy League, and the Liverpool groups managed by Brian Epstein, such as The Foremost and Gerry & The Pacemakers. During the summer holidays, schoolkids would flock to Denmark Street to try to get the autographs of their rock & roll heroes. It really was exciting to be there. In our parlance of the day, it was really "happening."

And on that Monday in 1964, I became a part of this scene. Paxton's was on Old Compton Street, just around the corner from Denmark Street. My job was to go all around Denmark Street picking up and delivering sheet music to the publishers and recording studios. Serving as an errand boy may not seem like the glamorous side of rock & roll, but if you think about it, it was the perfect situation for a fan. I could go just about anywhere I wanted, and I was hardly noticed by anyone. I would walk into a client's building and see Donovan in someone's office, or pass Roger Daltry on the street, or go to lunch at the Gioconda and see members of The Kinks sitting at the next table. It was just magical. It made me feel like a real insider. Of course, I was too young and shy and starstruck to actually speak to these luminaries and, as a "member of the industry," I was too proud to ask for their autographs, but it was an electric feeling just the same.

In my first days there, a guy from the company took me around to all of our clients and introduced me to the people working in the dispatch areas of each. One of our regular customers was Mills Music, and on that first visit he introduced me to the tea boy there, a tubby young fellow with thick glasses named Reg Dwight. I was endeared to him right away because he offered to make us a cup of tea even though I was just an office boy myself. We took him up on his offer, and we spent about half an hour chitchatting. He was very, very funny, constantly cracking jokes. My collegue and I sat there talking and enjoying his personality while he ran around the room pulling together all the music he had to deliver.

In the course of making my rounds, I'd see

Reg two or three times a week. He'd always make me a cup of tea and he'd always make me laugh, so I always looked forward to visiting with him. We were about the same age—he was a year and a half older than me, but he looked young for his age. We'd both dropped out of school to enter the music business and we were both musicians—he was a pianist and I was a guitarist. We also discovered that we both had fathers who had often been away from home—mine a touring musician, his in the military—fathers who had left home for good while we were both young. With all this in common, it's no wonder we became friends.

Being a teenage boy, I gave Reg a lot of good-natured ribbing. I used to call him "Billy Bunter" after a cartoon character we grew up with in England in the '50s. Billy Bunter was chubby and wore thick-rimmed glasses, just like Reg, and he had that same kind of self-deprecating personality that made it so easy to tease him. Reg had this pug nose that didn't hold his glasses up very well, so he was constantly wrinkling his nose to push them back up, or pushing them up with his hand. And because he was always joking around and was sort of a smart aleck himself, it was just natural to joke around with him. If my teasing ever bothered him—and I'm sure it did at times—he never showed it. In spite of all the joking around, we were friends.

One day I bumped into Reg on Denmark Street and he told me he'd formed a band. I knew that he had gone to the Royal Academy of Music on a youth scholarship and that he was playing piano in a local pub on Saturday nights, but it was hard for me to picture little Billy Bunter playing with a real band up on a stage. So I just said, "Really?" He responded, "Yeah, what do you think of our name? It's Bluesology." Well, I just laughed out loud. "Bluesology" was the title of a piece by the Modern Jazz Quartet, and Django Rheinhardt had used it as the title cut on one of his albums. Being a jazz buff —and having an honest claim to it because of my father and grandfather—I thought little Billy Bunter was being a bit pretentious. I said, "Pshaw! Bluesology! You must be joking!" He wasn't joking at all, and it was obvious that I'd hurt his feelings. Still, I didn't apologize, because I really did think he was being pretentious. It wasn't until later I learned that he also had an honest claim to serious musicianship.

    I had been at Paxton's for less than a year when a friend at another music publishing company, Francis, Day & Hunter, tipped me off about an opening for a tea boy at Dick James Music. Anything going on at Dick James Music caught people's attention, because they published The Beatles' music. Dick James himself had been a mildly successful singer in the big band days of the '40s and '50s, and he was best known to my generation as the vocalist on the theme song to *The Adventures of Robin Hood*, a popular British television show in the '50s. The story was that he had lucked into publishing the music of The Beatles when another publisher was late for an appointment with their manager, Brian Epstein. Regardless of how it happened, in 1965 the idea of working with any company associated with The Beatles was desirable.

My friend at Francis, Day & Hunter even knew the name of the secretary at Dick James Music, Lee Perry. So I went to the DJM offices, which were just around the corner from Denmark Street at 71-75 New Oxford Street. Lee Perry took me around to the administrator who, of course, knew all about my father. So he took me in to meet Dick James himself.

"You're Cab Kaye's son?" Mr. James asked.

"Yes," I said, and with that I was hired.

I started as a tea boy, which was a step down even from being an office boy. A tea boy, as the name implies, makes tea, cleans up around the office, and runs various errands—what Americans call a "gopher." But I started with an unusual level of respect because of my father's reputation, and by then I was pretty good at the guitar. It wasn't long before people around the office knew that I had an ear for music and that I could even compose songs. I was eager to learn all aspects of the music business, and I was always asking questions. It became obvious that I was, as we said in England, "keen to get on," to make something of myself. So when Dick James decided to build his own recording studio the next year, I ended up as studio manager at the ripe old age of seventeen.

With the money pouring in from the publication of The Beatles' music, Mr. James could afford to add a studio, and he did so with the intention of starting his own record label. With this in mind, he purchased a four-track recorder. (That means we could record four separate tracks of music and vocals, then layer them on top of one another on the final master tape). Unfortunately, some studios were already six-track, and within a year the first eight-track machines came out, so the studio at Dick James Music ended up recording mostly demos. Still, as you'll see, at least one batch of those demos played an important role in the history of rock & roll.

At first, Dick's son, Stephen James, was running the studio. But Stephen was being groomed to take over the company whenever his father retired, so he was being trained in more of an administrative role. In addition, he wasn't a musician, and I was already sitting in on some demo sessions as a guitarist, so Stephen turned it over to me. As studio manager and a session player, it was a small step to engineering and even producing the demos. So here I was, seventeen years old and a studio manager, session musician, engineer, and producer, all within two years of entering the music business.

Later, when DJM started its own record label, I added A&R ("Artist & Repertoire") to my lengthening list of experiences. (A&R men scout new talent, keep the existing talent happy, and basically manage the roster of artists signed to the record label.) Obviously, DJM was my university —that's where I learned my craft. Being a young, driven person who had aspired to the music business, it was an incredible experience for me to be plugged in to that degree. Those were good times.

Now, you may say, "Yeah, but you were only recording demos, so it's not that big a deal." But we're talking about demos for groups like The Hollies (most famous for "Bus Stop," "Long Cool Woman in a Black Dress," and "The Air That I Breathe") and all the groups signed to Brian Epstein's management company, NEMS Enterprises, such as Gerry & The Pacemakers, The Foremost, and Billy J. Kramer & The Dakotas. All these acts were walking into my little domain on a daily basis. I was directing them, playing on their demos, and having a pint of ale at the pub with them afterwards. Just imagine!

It wasn't long before I was playing as a session musician on the final recordings of their albums, as well, and the contacts made there led to session work for others. I began working through a contractor by the name of David Katz. At one point, I was running around to all the studios in London doing anywhere from three to five sessions a day, six or seven days a week. I was also playing with bands in their live performances, as well as being studio manager at DJM, so I was always working on several projects at once.

It was through my session work that I was introduced to Mick Jagger, and it was Mick Jagger who introduced me to drugs. Andrew Loog Oldham, the manager of The Rolling Stones, had his offices right next door to Dick James Music. My friend Billy Nichols worked for Oldham's record label, Immediate Records (the first independent record label), and he brought me in to play on an album Oldham was producing. Later, Oldham brought me back over to play on the debut album of a singer named P.P. Arnold. She had been one of the Ikettes—one of Ike & Tina Turner's backup singers—and her album was being produced by Mick Jagger.

At the time, Mick was dating Marianne Faithfull, a singer who had been discovered by Oldham and whose biggest hit, "As Tears Go By," had been written by The Stones. Mick and Marianne had an apartment in Marylebone Road. I went over there one afternoon to discuss the project, and when I got there, Jagger and a bunch of other guys were sitting around smoking hashish. For those who don't know, hashish—called "hash" for short—is a distillation of marijuana that is much more potent than just smoking the plant itself. It comes in a block that you crumble up and smoke in a pipe.

When I walked in, Mick held the pipe out to me and said, "Caleb, you gotta try this." I took it without thinking much about it. As a child, I had watched my father and his band smoking pot, and as a result of my time on Denmark Street, I knew that all the big names in the music business took drugs. I just thought, "Well, if this is what you need to do to play well, and if this is what you have to do to be famous, here goes."

Well, I went out of mind for about four hours. I thought I'd found God. For the next several years, I practiced what could realistically be called "recreational" drug use, but it wasn't long before I became a hardcore drug user. Of course, like any addict, I would have told you that I could quit anytime I wanted.

The Beatles were recording over at EMI Studios, which would be renamed Abbey Road Studios after their 1970 album made it famous. Because Dick James was their publisher, they dropped by DJM every now and then for a business meeting, but they weren't there on a regular basis. They certainly didn't use the DJM studios to cut demos—they were big enough that they didn't even have to go through the demo process. They had all the studio time they wanted to work out their songs. Nevertheless, I did play a small role in the Beatles story.

One day in November 1966, we got word that the "Fab Four" wanted to use the DJM studios to cut their annual Christmas single for the members of their fan club. These fan club recordings were usually just the four of them clowning around in the studio, but it was still pretty exciting to have John, Paul, George, and Ringo coming in. To my surprise, they brought legendary producer George Martin and studio engineer Geoff Emerick along with them. Why they let me run the sound board I'll never know—I was just seventeen years old with less than a year's experience running the studio. Beatles manager Brian Epstein was also there, and they all crowded into the tiny control room, hovering over me while the Beatles joked around in the studio. It was nerve-wracking at first, but the Beatles had planned out what they wanted to do, everything went without a hitch, and we all had fun doing it.

Paul McCartney must have liked the idea of a studio away from Abbey Road, because I ended up doing quite a bit of demo work for various side projects he was involved in. I'll never forget one incident that occurred in June 1967. We were working on a project for his brother Mike, who went by the stage name Mike McGear. Mike was in a musical comedy troupe called The Scaffold, and Paul was helping them get off the ground. The first morning of these sessions, I woke up and looked at the newspaper, and the headline read, "McCartney Admits Beatles Tried LSD." I thought, "Hold on. I'm in the studio with McCartney today." In fact, I was supposed to be at the studio in about an hour, and here he was on the front page of the paper admitting illegal activity. I knew it was going to be a strange day.

For those who weren't around back then, it's difficult to understand the impact of the situation. Drugs today are so widespread, and they're talked about so much, that it's difficult to remember a day when they were looked upon by the average person with something approaching real horror. I mean, today it would get more attention for a rock star to claim he *didn't* do drugs, but back then drugs were still viewed as a very real evil and as a very real threat to young people (as they have indeed turned out to be). Just a year or so earlier, The Byrds had seen their song "Eight Miles High" dropped from the play list of most radio stations because of its veiled drug references. As late as 1972, when Elton John released the song "Rocket Man," there was some controversy because of its use of the phrase "high as a kite."

You also have to understand the position held by The Beatles at that time. They were a social force unlike anything the music industry has produced before or since. Whether they liked it or not, they were the role models for England's and America's youth during a period of turbulent social change. The very fact that they had tried LSD meant that thousands of teenagers would feel justified in doing the same thing. (I know—I was a teenager myself.) Until that time, no celebrity had ever publicly admitted to drug use, unless they had been caught.

As Paul McCartney would point out later, he did not say that The Beatles were using LSD, only that they had tried it once, and he certainly didn't say that they endorsed it. Still, his candid and casual response to a reporter's question certainly suggested that he didn't think it was anything to hide, a shocking new attitude at the time.

I got dressed and headed down to DJM, and when I walked out of the tube station I could see a crowd of people around the studio entrance. As I got closer, I saw that it was all press people who were fighting to try to get into the studio. Here I was, trying to push my way through this crowd, sayng, "Excuse me, I have to get through. I'm the engineer for this session." It was absolute bedlam. Brian Epstein's people were there, working hard to keep these people out. I remember seeing Mal Evans and some of The Beatles' roadies there, clearing a way for me to get inside. When I walked into the studio, there was McCartney, sitting on a stool, dressed in a caftan, playing an acoustic guitar, just as calm as he could be. It was as if he were totally unaware of the huge controversy swirling around him. We conducted the session like any other, but I don't mind telling you it took me awhile to get fully focused.

My most exciting Beatles-related incident occurred later that year, and it resulted from an unexpected perk that came with my job. As a music publisher, it was DJM's job to produce the sheet music for forthcoming albums, both to protect against copyright infringement and to try to sell the songs to other artists. You may be surprised to learn that the artists themselves do not supply sheet music to the publishing houses, for the simple reason that very few popular songs are ever written out. They are usually the result of one or more musicians jamming together, then practicing a few times, then playing the song in the studio. Few rock artists even know how to write out sheet music.

So how is sheet music produced? A guy called a "copyist" listens to the album, figures out what notes and chords are being played, and transcribes them onto sheet music. That's how it was done back then, and that's how it's done today. At that time, there was an older guy on Denmark Street named Jeff Muston who was a free-lance copyist for a variety of publishing houses. He was the copyist who did all The Beatles' music. He had a dingy little basement office on Denmark Street. I would take a copy of the album's master tapes over to him and he would write out the music for it. Jeff was a piano player, so he sometimes had a little trouble with guitar chords, and many times he called me up and said, "Hey, Caleb, could you come over here and tell me just what the heck this chord is that these guys are playing?" So I even had a hand in figuring out some of The Beatles' sheet music. I remember specifically helping him on some of the songs on the *Help!* soundtrack, *Rubber*

Soul, and *Revolver.*

Because the sheet music helped protect the copyright, the publishing house had to have it out before the album was released. In order to do this, the publishing house had to have a copy of the master recording of each album as soon as it was available. The tapes were brought to me the moment they were finished, which meant that I was often the first person outside the various recording studios to hear the albums of The Hollies, The Beatles, and many other groups. This perk was quite a bonus to a young man who was crazy about rock & roll.

In the case of The Beatles, Geoff Emerick would have the tapes sent over under heightened security and with great secrecy. We hadn't yet coined the term "bootleg," but even then it was of utmost importance that no unauthorized copies of the albums would leak out prior to their official release. So one night in 1967, under cover of darkness, I was delivered a copy of the master tapes of an album called *Sgt. Pepper's Lonely Hearts Club Band*. This revolutionary album had been much anticipated and, as far as I know, I got to hear the finished product before anyone other than George Martin and The Beatles themselves.

It's been well documented that *Sgt. Pepper* had a profound effect on many rock artists, most notably Brian Wilson of The Beach Boys, whose long slide into seclusion was hastened by an obsessive drive to equal that effort. As I listened to the album alone at night in the stillness of the DJM studios, it had a profound effect on me, as well. Like so many musicians of the day, I recognized in the first listen that these four "lads from Liverpool" had managed to merge popular music with art, to lift it out of the realm of teenyboppers and into the realm of adults, and to raise the standard so high that things would never be the same again.

There were very strict rules against playing these tapes for anyone, but that night I knew that I was sitting on something bigger than any rules. I called Graham Nash of The Hollies, and he came over to the studio and listened while I played the tapes for him. I remember watching him as the music poured out of those big studio speakers. It was obvious that listening to these tapes was like a religious experience for him. In most cases, a person in this situation would want to hear it a second time right away. But Graham just listened silently, and when it ended, he stood up, shook his head and said, "They've done it." Then he said again, "They've done it." And without another word he walked out of the studio. The next year, Graham quit The Hollies to join up as part of Crosby, Stills & Nash. I never asked him about it, but I have the feeling that, like many other artists, *Sgt. Pepper* made him realize he'd gone as far as he could go in a certain direction.

Perhaps the most exciting thing about that period was being a part of the major changes the recording industry was going through. When I first started doing studio work in 1965, demos were still being recorded mono or straight to stereo. A lot of records were still recorded live, meaning that the band all went into the studio and played together. The vocalist would be in a booth singing live while the guitarists and drummers were playing along in real time. If anyone made a single mistake—the vocalist catching his breath, the drummer missing a beat—the whole thing had to start over. Even very complicated guitar solos had to be recorded live.

The two-, three-, and even four-track recording machines allowed you to do overdubs, which helped immensely. You could record the vocals on one track until you got them right, then layer them over the recordings of the instruments. But you were still greatly limited in the final sound you could achieve in a recording studio. Even back when bands were still playing that straight-forward style of rock & roll from the '50s, you had the main vocalist, background vocals, drums, two or three guitars, other instruments such as a piano, and often some sort of accompaniment such as a string section. So even four tracks weren't enough to give everyone their own separate recording.

Furthermore, if you had a drummer playing in the same room with the guitarists, the drums would be picked up not only by the drummer's microphones, but also by the guitarists' microphones, a problem known as "bleed." The same was true of other instruments and of vocals. So we had to partition people off or even put them in separate rooms with microphone wires running through the walls, and still we would spend a great deal of time avoiding bleed and getting through a take with no mistakes.

Around 1967, eight-track recording was developed. A good friend of mine, Keith Grant, was the owner of Olympic Studios, which was over on George Street at that time, and which later moved to the southern part of the city to a place called Barnes. Keith had the first eight-track studio in England, and I was invited along with a lot of other musicians to come and hear this new system. Well, we all thought we'd died and gone to heaven, listening to these four extra tracks. People were saying, "Oh, you can put the kick in the middle and the snare on the left and the high-hat over here, and the toms from left to right." We all thought this was incredible.

It was no coincidence that, about this time,

The Beatles and others began experimenting with all kinds of weird sounds and layering on instruments previously unheard on rock songs. The technology made it possible, right in time for the psychedelic phase of music prompted by the hippie subculture of that era. But if you could have eight tracks, why not sixteen? By the early '70s, we were recording everything in sixteen-track, and by the end of the decade it was thirty-two. Today, all major studios use recorders with at least forty-eight tracks, and many have eighty or more tracks. This is just one way that technology has made possible a lot of the music we've heard since those early, unsophisticated days.

Another man I knew back then, Pepe Rush, invented the fuzzbox for guitars, which he called the Tonebender. With this, you could get some really weird sounds out of your guitar. That was important because, back then, everything was still analog, meaning that it was recorded in real time onto magnetic tape. If you wanted to make an unusual sound, you had to figure out a way to produce it for the recorder, or you had to do some odd things with the tape itself. When John Lennon was putting together "Revolution #9" for the White Album, he took various recordings, cut them into little strips, and spliced them back together in a random fashion. (And all the stoned hippies of the day spent hours trying to figure out the "messages" in Lennon's music!) And, of course, The Beatles and many others experimented with "backwards masking," which was achieved simply by turning the tape over when recording, then placing it on the machine in the proper way when playing it back.

Once digital recording came along in the '80s, all that changed. With digital recording, sounds can be manipulated after they've been recorded. They can be played back, doubled and tripled, distorted, and altered for all kinds of special effects. And with the MIDI systems now being used, which hook computerized synthesizers up to instruments, a piano key can be used to produce the sound of another instrument or some special effect even during a live performance.

But the changes occurring back in the 1960s weren't just technological. Rock & roll was becoming a cultural force, and it was drawing increased energy as the music of a generation that was striking out for freedom and that looked to music for the first time as a powerful means of social commentary. This was true not just in the lyrics of the day, but in the very form of the music —folk rock, acid rock, and psychedelic rock.

I remember going to the Saville Theatre, which was owned by Brian Epstein, to see Jimi Hendrix. This was a pivotal event in the London music scene. Every guitar player in the business showed up to see Hendrix, and it was as if he taught us all how to play guitar all over again. I remember that people left in complete silence. Like listening to *Sgt. Pepper* for the first time, it was almost like a religious experience to us, or the closest thing to it in our secular world. We all had our jaws on the floor, because none of us had ever seen anyone play guitar like that. Just after that, Eric Clapton bought a Fender Stratocaster, and soon everyone was playing the Strat and imitating Hendrix's style. We all went back to square one.

In short, I was there when rock & roll was coming into its own both artistically and technologically. I was there when it firmly established itself as a cultural force and the voice of a generation. Over the next ten years, these changes would bring money, glitz, arena-sized concerts, groupies, drugs, and an emphasis on promotion over product. I didn't know it at the time, but popular music was about to change from a cottage industry to a massive juggernaut of noise and energy and glamour, and it was about to sweep me along with it. Because, without realizing it, I was about to attach myself to the one performer who would come

to embody rock & roll in the following decade.

Chapter Four

The Great Purge

When I first moved to Dick James Music, I didn't see my friend Reg Dwight for possibly a year or so. His band Bluesology, whose name I had laughed at, had been doing pretty well on the club circuit. They had released several singles on the Phillips label, and Reg had performed lead vocals on two of them. The band had established such a strong reputation that it was providing backup for the European tours of American artists such as Little Richard, Patti LaBelle, The Drifters, and The Ink Spots. Then word came that Bluesology had signed on as the permanent backing band for singer Long John Baldry.

One day in June of 1967, Reg showed up at the DJM studios to do some demos. He had lost some weight and grown his hair out, so he looked a lot less like Billy Bunter, but there was no mistaking my little friend. When he saw me walk in, I'm sure he was petrified, thinking, "Oh, my goodness, he's going to make fun of me again." But his band had proven itself respectable (if not completely worthy of its name), and I'm proud to say I behaved myself.

Reg had been brought there by another young man named Ray Williams, the talent scout for Liberty Records, an American label that had been using EMI as its European distributor, but which had now decided to establish full operations in England. As I learned later, Ray had placed an ad for new talent in *New Musical Express* magazine, and Reg had turned up to audition. He had grown disenchanted with what he perceived to be a lack of ambition among the members of Bluesology, and once the band signed on to back up Long John Baldry, he began quietly looking for something else.

He had applied to Liberty as a songwriter as well as a vocalist and keyboard player. While Ray had not signed him to Liberty Records, he did see enough potential to start working with him. He brought Reg in to DJM to see if we might be interested in him.

It was obvious that Reg was serious about this effort, so we set about trying him on a few songs. His keyboard playing was fine, but when he started to sing, it was in this clear, high voice that reminded me of Sandie Shaw. Sandie was a female pop singer at the time who was famous for singing in bare feet.

As we listened to the playback, we all agreed that his tunes were quite competent, but that the vocals needed some work. We also agreed that his lyrics were weak and that he needed a lyricist. At that time, we were mainly thinking of him in terms of being a songwriter, a session musician, and perhaps the keyboard player and vocalist in a band, but certainly not as a solo act.

Ray Williams, in addition to signing talent to the Liberty label, had been shrewdly signing artists to management deals and publishing deals through GRALTO, the publishing entity that was a joint venture between The Hollies and Dick James

Music. He hooked Reg up with two other songwriters he had under contract through GRALTO, Nicky James and Kirk Duncan. He also gave him some lyrics that had been sent in by a young man from Lincolnshire in response to the same ad.

As studio manager, I had been letting songwriters and aspiring artists record demos after hours at no charge. I justified this by telling myself that Dick James would ultimately profit from any successful songs or acts that emerged from these late-night sessions. But, in my youthful enthusiasm, I carried things too far. I would actually rent equipment or book string sections to complete a recording, requisitioning the checks under my own authority. It was only a matter of time before I would be caught, but in the meantime, what fun we were having!

So I began to work with Reg on a regular basis, recording demos of the songs he had written. After a long day of recording and playing, a group of us would meet up there in the evening and work on each other's demos. Reg would play keyboards on a demo for The Mirage, then the members of The Mirage—including a young bass player named Dee Murray—would play on one of Reg's demos. I would set the volume levels in the control room, then come around to play guitar on the recordings. When we'd finish, we'd all go out for a late-night meal at Wimpy's.

In fact, we all spent so much time in that little studio at DJM that we began to refer to it jokingly as "The Gaff," British slang for a flat, or apartment. After all, we practically lived there. And during almost every session, the air would be thick with marijuana smoke.

It was during this period that my friendship with Reg really kicked in. That's when we started hanging out together and going to record stores together and being real buddies. We were interested in the same kind of music and we both dreamed of making music ourselves. Most importantly, though, as our friendship grew, we began to fully realize how we had been affected by our fathers' rejection and abandonment. These issues connected us even more strongly, and pretty soon we were staying at each other's houses and getting to know each other's families.

Reg's mum especially liked me, partially, I think, because she saw my calm demeanor as a counterbalance to her son's eccentric moodiness. We'd be sitting at supper, and the conversation would naturally turn to the music business. Suddenly, Reg would jump up, throw a jacket around his shoulders movie-star style, and start shouting, "I'm going to be star, do you hear me? A *star!*" Off he'd go down the hallway, his muffled shouts still emerging from his bedroom in the back. His mum would look at me with her worried eyes and say, "Oh, Caleb, can't you say something to him?" I would laugh, then get up to go bring my buddy back to what we then thought was reality. Little did we know that his funny little rants would turn out to be true.

One day in July 1967, while Reg was playing keyboards in a recording session and I was in the control room, I turned around to see a young man sitting there wearing sunglasses and a jacket that was at least one size too small. He looked like he had just stepped off the farm. I said, "Are you supposed to be here?" Ray Williams explained to me that he was the young man from Lincolnshire whose lyrics Reg had been writing music to. He *had* just stepped off the farm! His name was Bernie Taupin.

When Reg came out of the session, he was introduced to Bernie, and the two went out for a cup of coffee. They struck up a friendship immediately, and soon Bernie was joining us when we ran around together, visiting the record stores, listening to records at Reg's mum's house. It soon became apparent that Reg had found his lyric-writer. Bernie's lyrics were pretentious, juvenile, and infused with references to mysticism and rural life, but that was all in keeping with the esoteric, fantasy-laden, at-one-with-the-universe atmosphere of the hippie subculture of the day. And when Reg put his music and his voice to those lyrics, something happened. What and why are unexplainable, but there was no denying that the songs they began to produce together had a unique and even haunting quality about them.

Reg began working exclusively with Bernie and even invited him to move in to his mum's house, although Bernie would still take the train back up to Lincolnshire on the weekends. So now

Bernie would be sitting in on the after-hours demo sessions as well, and it was usually he, Reg, and I who went out together for an early morning snack afterwards.

Within several months, we had produced a couple of dozen demo songs written by Reg and Bernie. Then the roof fell in.

It's still referred to today as "The Great Purge." It nearly cost me my job and stopped Reg and Bernie's songwriting careers before they started. Instead, in the mysterious way in which God often works, it kick-started those careers.

One night we were in the middle of a recording session when I looked up to see Ronnie Brohn standing in the doorway. Ronnie was the company's business manager. He was a member of the old guard at DJM, a very straight-laced and humorless fellow, and not the kind to take kindly to the unauthorized use of the studio facilities. We all froze.

"What's going on here?" he demanded. We sort of looked at each other and didn't say anything for a moment, always a clear indication of guilt.

"It's a recording session," I said, trying nonchalantly to wave away the smoke from the joint I was holding.

"Does Dick know about this?" he shot back. The answer was obvious before I managed to stammer out a response.

"Right. I'm telling Dick," he said. He turned and stormed out.

Needless to say, the recording session ended

then and there. I remember thinking, as I turned out the lights, that this may be the last time I would ever see that studio, and, perhaps, any studio.

Remember, I was still an eighteen-year-old kid at this time, and I was about to be called on the carpet by the single most successful music publisher in England because I'd been spending his money without his authorization. Being fired from Dick James Music under such circumstances probably meant that I would never work in the music industry again.

I spent a restless night that night. I might get away with the after-hours studio time, I reasoned, but there was no defense for requisitioning those checks. Worse, much of the time and money had gone for Reg's demos, and Reg wasn't even signed to DJM. In fact, he was signed to GRALTO only through a nebulous arrangement with Ray Williams. I just assumed I was about to lose my job.

When I got into the office the next morning, Ronnie Brohn had done all he could to stir up a hornet's nest. The secretary warned me as soon as I walked in the door. Stephen James has said in interviews that he spoke to me first, and he may well have, but what I remember is being called in to see Dick James himself and thinking, "Well, this is it." Mr. James had some of the figures regarding my check requisitions in front of him, gladly supplied, I'm sure, by Mr. Brohn. There was no question that he was angry.

"Okay, what's been going on in the studio?"

he demanded. I told him I was just trying to give some guys a break, and I started to spin out my rationalization about DJM ultimately profiting from anything that emerged from these sessions. If he heard that part, he didn't act like it.

"And these sessions have been going on after hours?"

"Yes, sir," I said.

"Who are they? I want to know who they are." So I ran down a short list of those who had been using the studio.

"That's it—I'm throwing them all out," he said. "It's over."

The next thing out of his mouth was probably going to be that it was over for me, as well. Instinctively, I spoke up first.

"Well," I said, "you can throw them out and you can sack me if you want, but I've got these two guys that I think you ought to listen to their stuff." I was sincere (if ungrammatical) about this, but I'll have to admit that I had other reasons for saying it. First, it could only help my case that I was willing to sacrifice my own job for the sake of others. Second, Reg's demos were the best thing I had produced in those late-night sessions, and I thought it might save my skin if Mr. James knew that we hadn't just been wasting our time and his money.

"Who are they?" he asked.

I told him who they were and told him they had the same arrangement as Nicky James and Kirk Duncan, which wasn't exactly true because Bernie wasn't signed to anything. I offered to go get the tapes, and he said, "Okay," but in a tone that suggested that my fate was still undecided. I brought the tapes in, and I remember that I was actually sweating as I threaded the tape on the machine in his office. At that moment, I felt I would be fired if Dick James didn't like what he heard on this tape. He sat back and listened as I played him "Skyline Pigeon," "When I Was Tealby Abbey," "Watching the Planes Go By," and several others. After five or six songs, I stopped the tape and held my breath, but there was no hesitation on his part.

"That's great," he said. "I'm going to sign them." Just like that. I was sent out with a pretty clear understanding that henceforth I was to follow proper procedure, and later that afternoon two other frightened teenage boys were escorted into Mr. James's office. Reg and Bernie went in thinking they were in trouble and emerged with a songwriting contract that would pay them a whopping ten pounds a week apiece.

Once we got over our shock, we were ecstatic. Not only could we now work on their demos openly in the daylight, but they were even getting paid for it! We adjourned immediately and went for a curry at L'Orient—which Reg had renamed Leyton Orient after the football team. The harrowing experience of the Great Purge further solidified our friendship, and although Reg and Bernie had clearly become soulmates by this time, my friendship with Reg also grew stronger. Bernie was still taking the train back to Lincolnshire on the weekends, so Reg and I continued to spend lots of time together. When Bernie was in town, it was often the three of us together.

In fact, we became such close friends, and we were working together so well professionally, that we even began discussing linking up as a three-person songwriting team. The idea was for Bernie to write the lyrics, then Reg and I would compose the music and produce a demo. We were so keen on the idea that we had a publicity photo taken of the three of us, a photo that is now apparently lost to history.

Unfortunately, our initial excitement was short-lived. Despite having signed Reg and Bernie on the basis of songs written in their unique style, Dick James instructed the pair to write cute little pop songs (the kind he could sell to Lulu or Sandie Shaw) or big sentimental ballads (the kind he could sell to Tom Jones or Englebert Humperdinck). This was simply not the kind of song the two wanted to write, and it certainly wasn't the kind of song I was interested in producing and playing guitar on. The result was some really awful songs. Perhaps the worst was "Annabella," with its repeated rhyme of "Annabella, um-buh-rella," a direct rip-off of The Hollie's "Bus Stop" and another recent song called "Cinderella Rockafella." Dick James's persistence in this area would lead to some major problems in the coming months.

We didn't have much time to think about it at first, because in November 1967, just after Reg and Bernie had signed their contract, Long John

Baldry suddenly had a huge hit with a tear-jerker of a ballad called "Let the Heartaches Begin." This meant that Bluesology would now be backing him on the cabaret circuit, the Bailey Clubs and similar venues where people would be eating and talking while the band played. As far as Reg was concerned, that was the last straw, and he let Long John Baldry know that he wasn't going to be around much longer. Baldry got him to promise to stay on through the Christmas season.

    When Reg found out they needed another guitar player, he asked me if I would take the job so that he and I could work on his material while on the road. I think he also wanted me along as a friend who could help him look toward the future as a relief from the present. So I joined Bluesology for a brief stint of about four months, which was four months too long as far as I was concerned. Reg and I sat together on all the trips and roomed together at every hotel, still dreaming our teenage dreams together.

One bright spot in my brief stint with Bluesology was that on several occasions we opened for a band called Cream, which at that very moment was riding high on its first and greatest hit, "Sunshine of Your Love." The lead guitarist was a young wunderkind named Eric Clapton, whom I already admired from his work with John Mayall's Bluesbreakers. The other two members of Cream, drummer Ginger Baker and bassist Jack Bruce, had been in Alexis Korner's Blues, Inc. and The Graham Bond Organization. As you can tell by the names of these bands, they were serious, blues-oriented groups—my kind of music. Watching these guys at work was exciting; getting to know them backstage and after the shows was a thrill.

Up until that time, my dating life was probably not much different from that of any other teenager. I dated about the normal amount, and the dates were pretty traditional—dinner and a movie, nightclubbing with friends, going to a concert. Most of the women I met already knew people in the music industry, so my position wasn't something that was particularly impressive, and it wasn't like there were groupies hanging around dying to go out with studio engineers and session players. Even my introduction to sex was pretty much the norm for young boys out on their own in the world.

Things changed when I went on the road and became visible as a member of a band. Don't get me wrong; playing in the backing band for Long John Baldry in the Bailey Clubs didn't mean you got your own fan club, but it did put you at a special advantage when it came to meeting the "birds." I remember the first time it happened, just after I joined Bluesology. It was at the Cavendish Club in Sheffield in December 1967. I had just turned nineteen. I spotted this waitress from the stage, and after the show I approached her and started "chatting her up," as we called it, and soon we were back in my hotel room. Reg was there, pretending to be asleep, but giggling under his covers so loudly we couldn't help but hear him. This girl and I were so drunk we didn't care, and we went right on as if no one was there. That scene was repeated more than once while we were on the road with Bluesology.

A few nights later, on Christmas Eve of 1967, Reg also "hit pay dirt." At the Cavendish Club that night, there was a local deejay who happened to be a midget, and the woman he was with had to be at least six feet tall. After the show I noticed Reg talking to her—I noticed it because Reg was usually too shy to have an extended conversation with women. This woman seemed to tower over Reg almost as much as she did over her date, yet I noticed that he seemed relaxed. That night, for the first time, Reg and I both had company.

The next morning, on Christmas day, after

the girls had left, I remember that Reg gave me a pair of socks as a Christmas present, which is about all we could afford on our incomes. That touching gesture says volumes about Reg—he was the only one in the band who even thought about giving anyone a Christmas present.

Sheffield is about 200 miles north of London, but a couple of weeks after we played there, I received a letter from the girl I had met saying she had moved to London to be with me. At about the same time, the woman Reg had met, Linda, also moved to London to be with him. And we were just backup musicians! It was my first glimpse of what stardom can do to people.

After that, whenever I was playing up on stage, I would keep my eye out for my "target" for the evening, and when I approached them afterwards, they were almost invariably interested. Then, when we played to a college crowd in Cardiff, in Wales, things moved to a new level. The fact that Baldry had the number-one hit song at the moment meant little to the older crowds at the Bailey Clubs, but to the young people who actually listened to pop music, he was the hottest thing going. So at this club in Cardiff, these girls were screaming and jumping up and grabbing at my legs. Now, I had been raised on rock & roll, and we had all seen the films of Elvis and The Beatles, and I had witnessed some of this when I attended concerts, but this was the first time it had happened to me.

Again, I was just a hired guitarist, and these

kids didn't know me from Adam, yet they were getting all excited about just touching me. For a young man like me, it was a very heady feeling. I knew that it really had nothing to do with me personally, of course, but having women getting excited about just touching you would be pretty close to paradise for any teenage boy.

Meanwhile, Reg's frustration with playing in Baldry's shadow began to take on comic proportions. While Long John Baldry would be out front singing, Reg would make comments from his keyboards loud enough for the band members to hear, causing us to laugh. Then one night, while Baldry was talking to the audience, Reg left his electric organ and just started storming around the stage, cursing and complaining and even kicking his amplifier in full view of the audience. The rest of us were just beside ourselves with laughter. Baldry was rightfully angry, and he gave Reg a good talking to afterwards. Nevertheless, the next night, there was Reg stomping around the stage behind him. Remember, Reg was short and stocky, and his only stage costume at that time was this huge fur coat that made him look even stockier, so in the dimmed lights behind Baldry, the audience saw what must have looked like an angry Winnie-the-Pooh stalking around the stage destroying equipment.

As Bernie would later put it, Reg was "too hot for the band, with a desperate desire for change." The rest of the band got a lot of laughs out of it, though at Baldry's expense.

Meanwhile, an interesting thing was happening. When Stephen James took Reg and Bernie's demos around to try to sell the songs to other artists, the executives and managers kept turning the songs down because they were "too original," and several offered the opinion that the person singing on the demo had a good enough voice to release the songs himself. Dick James had built the studio that I managed because he wanted to start his own record label, and the obvious place to start was with the talent they already had under contract. So, just one month after Reg had been amazed to get a songwriting contract, he was even more amazed when Dick and Stephen James began talking about offering him a recording contract.

People today look at the nerdy pictures of

the young Reg Dwight and wonder how in the world anyone could have envisioned this young man as a potential rock star. These people are looking at very early pictures of Reg, and they are forgetting that everyone in the mid-'60s wore horn-rimmed glasses and straight-legged slacks. By the time Reg came into my studios in June 1967, he had lost weight, grown his hair longer, and adopted the mod clothes of the Carnaby Street style. Besides, pop music in the '60s had an integrity it did not have in the '50s—it was not based solely on fabricated pretty boys, but on sensitive souls who had something to say. If Bob Dylan, José Feliciano, and Simon and Garfunkel could sell millions of records, then looks and polish were no longer prerequisites to becoming a musical artist.

In addition, the plain and simple fact is that everyone liked Reg. He was funny, he was friendly, he was talented, and he wasn't at all egotistical. I think Dick James looked on him as sort of a son and was, therefore, willing to give him a chance to prove himself. Dick and Stephen James had listened to all the demos I had produced for Reg, and they recognized that he had the potential to develop as a serious artist. They also knew that he had aspirations to cut his own records, and Dick was a shrewd businessman. If one of his songwriters was going to cut records, why let him do it somewhere else?

Dick and Stephen asked that Reg cut an acceptable single before they actually signed a contract. This was a polite way of reminding us that they wanted the type of commercial pop song that Dick James could sell to other artists. While Reg was capable of producing nice little pop melodies at the drop of a hat, Bernie more strongly resisted compromising his poetic integrity by writing shallow lyrics. But Reg was desperate to get his career going, so while we were on the road with Bluesology, he wrote the lyrics and music to two songs—"I've Been Loving You" and "Here's To The Next Time."

In December 1967, between Bluesology gigs, we went into the studio and cut these two songs to be released as his first single. Reg felt guilty about leaving Bernie out of the picture, so he insisted that Bernie be credited on the record label. In keeping with Dick James' wishes—and against my natural inclinations—I produced these songs with that sort of over-the-top, big-ballad sound that Tom Jones and Englebert Humperdinck had popularized.

Despite the disagreement in styles, Reg was greatly encouraged by the possibility of a recording contract. He was feeling positive and confident, and I don't think it's just coincidence that he had landed his first real girlfriend during this time. On January 10, 1968, he signed a five-year recording contract with Dick James Music. The first single was scheduled for release through the Phillips label in early March. Once the contract was signed, Reg gave his notice to Baldry, and I let it be known that I would be leaving along with him. It was in late January or early February of 1968 that Reg and I played our last gig with Bluesology in Glasgow at a club called Green's Playhouse. Green's was notorious for its violence—there was a cage around the stage to protect the bands from flying beer bottles, coins, and spark plugs. (And you thought that scene in *The Blues Brothers* movie was just made up.)

On the flight home, Reg and I sat together as always. He was restless, and he was trying to decide what his stage name might be. He was adamant that "Reg" just wouldn't do. He'd always hated the name. "Sounds like a librarian's assistant," he would say. At the time there was a very famous British cyclist who had won the Tour de France named Reg Harris, so I used to kid Reg that his name sounded like a cyclist. We all agreed he would have to adopt a stage name, and all of us in the band—and Bernie, as well—had been thinking about it ever since Dick and Stephen had first started talking to him about a recording contract.

He had told me before that he liked the first name of Bluesology's saxophone player, Elton Dean. Although I didn't know it, Dean has since said that Reg came to him during that flight and asked if he would mind if Reg called himself Elton Dean. Naturally, Dean was a bit taken aback by that, so Reg looked around at the other band members, and his eyes lighted on Long John Baldry himself. I remember Reg nudging me at one point in the flight and showing me the name he had written on a piece of paper. "How do you like that?" he asked. I said I thought it sounded great, and the decision was made. To the record-buying public, my little friend would not be known as Reg Dwight. He would be known as Elton John.

Chapter Five

The Butterfly Emerges

We all looked at Reg's new name as a stage name—nothing more and nothing less. We had grown up in an era of pop acts with obvious stage names like Brenda Lee (who was born Brenda Tarpley), Doris Day (who was born Doris Kappelhoff), and Little Richard (whose full name is Richard Penniman). Long before Prince and Madonna thought of calling themselves by their first names only, we had Dion and Fabian. And the obvious stage name of Chubby Checkers (Ernest Evans) was a play on the stage name of Fats Domino (who could at least claim that his last name really was Domino).

Despite the ostensible earnestness of the musicians of the '60s, stage names were no less common in that era. Bob Dylan had been born Robert Allen Zimmerman, Joni Mitchell was really Roberta Joan Anderson, and Van Morrison was really George Ivan. "Herman" of Herman's Hermits was actually Peter Noone.

Stage names have continued unabated in the music industry to the present day. In the '70s, we had Eddie Money (Edward Mahoney), Gilbert O'Sullivan (Raymond O'Sullivan), Lobo (Roland Kent Lavoie), Dr. John (Malcolm Rebennack), and Dr. Hook (Ray Sawyer). In the '80s, we had Boy George (George O'Dowd), Adam Ant (Stuart Goddard), George Michael (Georgios Kyriacos Panayiotou), and Taylor Dayne (Leslie

Wonderman). In the '90s, we had Babyface (Kenneth Edmonds), Dr. Dre (Andre Young), Salt-N-Pepa (Cheryl James and Sandra Denton), Coolio (Artis Ivey), and Seal (Sealhenry Samuel). Since then we've had Eminem (Marshall Bruce Mathers III), 50 Cent (Curtis James Jackson III), Nelly (Cornell Iral Haynes, Jr.), Pink (Alecia Beth Moore), and Lady Gaga (Stefani Joanne Angelina Germanotta).

And, of course, the single-name-only game continues, as well. There were Cher, Lulu, and Donavan in the '60s; Melanie and Sting in the '70s; Madonna, Prince, and Sade in the '80s; and Jewel, Monica, and Brandy in the '90s. Since then, we've had Usher, Adele, Drake, Rihanna, Kesha, and Fergie.

Prince turned the stage name into self-parody when he changed his already-pretentious moniker into an unpronounceable symbol in the early '90s, prompting everyone in the industry to refer to him first as "The Artist Formerly Known as Prince" and then simply as "The Artist." The fact that otherwise intelligent and influential people would go along with such a charade says a lot about the music industry.

In our eyes, stage names were a regular part of the business. One of Reg and Bernie's early songs, "I Can't Go On Living Without You," was sung in the Eurovision contest by Lulu, who was actually Marie McDonald McLaughlin Lawrie. Even Kiki Dee, who was a backup singer in London at the time and who would later have a monster hit with Elton dueting on "Don't Go Breaking My Heart," was actually Pauline Matthews. "Elton John" was just one more stage name, and Reg Dwight was still Reg Dwight as far as we were all concerned.

All of us, that is, except Reg himself. Reg saw his old name as symbolic of his old life and his old persona, and he hated both. (Later, in the autobiographical song "Captain Fantastic and the Brown Dirt Cowboy," Bernie Taupin ingeniously summarized the frustration of Elton's early life with the single word "regimented," a play on both Reg's name and his strict upbringing at the hand of his military father.) The new name—along with the recording contract and his new girlfriend—were the first stages of a metamorphosis that would change

Reg beyond recognition in the coming years.

It was in January 1968 that Reg's girlfriend Linda followed him from Sheffield, and they moved in together, along with Bernie, into a flat on Furlong Road in Islington. Reg and Bernie were soon complaining about her domineering ways. The boys complained that Linda refused to cook for them as Reg's mum had done, although Linda has since denied this. I didn't go over to that flat many times, but I do remember that Linda's ratty little dogs used to leave their "calling cards" all over the floor.

The main thing I remember about the whole affair was how ridiculous Reg and Linda looked together, and you really had to make an effort to look ridiculous to someone in the music industry in

1968. Linda was tall and thin—over six feet tall—while Reg was only 5' 8" and stocky. Linda had a snooty, upper-class air about her and she dressed in high-fashion clothes, while Reg was trying to dress like a rock star, which is a bit difficult when you have no money. His favorite piece of apparel at that time was that huge fur coat that made him appear to be as wide as he was tall. The two of them together were a sight to see. If ever there was one of those situations where you would say, "What's wrong with this picture?", this was it.

One day the three of us went to lunch together, and as we started walking back to the studio, they were in front of me, and I got tickled looking at them. Here was Linda, tall and thin, and here was stocky Reg wearing his enormous fur coat, and here were Linda's little dogs down at the end of the leash that Reg was holding. Looking at them, I realized they formed the numeral "10." I just fell against a lampost in hysterics.

Reg knew they looked ridiculous, and I think he sort of liked the teasing I gave him about it. I would see them together and smile or chuckle, and he would cut me this funny sideways look that let me know he was in on the joke. Linda, on the other hand, was not amused.

My friendship and my professional work with Reg went on uninterrupted, but Linda didn't share our wacky senses of humor, so she never became part of the group. While it's true that Linda attended many of our late-night practice and recording sessions, it soon became obvious that their physical differences were merely symbolic of much deeper differences. I didn't dislike her particularly, but I certainly felt that she was distracting Reg from what we were trying to do. Bernie was getting increasingly frustrated with their living arrangements. I knew that Reg wasn't completely happy, either, but he was letting himself get pulled further and further in. As young girls will often do, Linda began to pressure Reg into marriage, and in the early summer of 1968, he told us all that they would be getting married on June 22nd.

I knew that Reg didn't want to get married, but he was afraid to break things off. For one thing, like many people before and since, he had not considered the difficulty of breaking up with someone you live with. To top it off, she had reportedly told him she was pregnant, which wasn't true. Reg's angst climaxed in his famous comical suicide attempt, in which he turned on the gas stove in their flat, but opened all the windows and got a pillow to cushion his head as it lay on the oven door. Finally, just before the wedding, during a night out at the clubs that I missed, Long John Baldry talked Reg into breaking things off. The breakup was as difficult as Reg had expected, and the next morning his stepfather came to pick him and Bernie up, taking them and their belongings back to Reg's bedroom at his mother's flat in Pinner.

  Later, Elton and Bernie immortalized the relationship in the 1975 Top Ten hit, "Someone Saved My Life Tonight." While I have no right to speak for Elton and how this particular relationship affected him, I do feel that this song has built the story up in the public mind perhaps more than it deserves. You have to remember that we were teenage boys at the time, and like all teenage boys, there were girlfriends in and out of all our lives. As far as I was concerned, Linda was just one more girlfriend that didn't work out. In fact, Reg and Linda lasted exactly six months, which is probably about the average length of a teenage romance. No one was forcing Reg to date her or to live with her, so one could argue that the song is unfairly hard on her. (Remember that the lyrics to the song were written by Bernie, who apparently felt he had an ax to grind with her.)

I'm sure the whole situation was a traumatic

and memorable experience for Reg, but it took place when all of us—Linda included—were young and immature. Don't we all have at least one immature relationship from our adolescent years that we would just as soon forget?

By this time, DJM had succeeded in selling several of Reg and Bernie's songs. Roger Cook and Roger Greenaway, who had earlier had hits under the stage names Jonathan & David, purchased the rights to "Skyline Pigeon." A DJM group called Plastic Penny, whose lead vocalist was a young drummer named Nigel Olsson, covered "Turn to Me." And, as I mentioned, Lulu (best known in America for her 1967 hit, "To Sir With Love") sang "I Can't Go on Living Without You" in the Eurovision song contest. Unfortunately, the smattering of sales weren't enough to justify a songwriting contract on an indefinite basis. And when Elton's first single had been released in March 1968, it sank without a trace.

The problem was a simple one. With the exception of "Skyline Pigeon," these songs were written to fulfill Dick James's mandate to produce more "commercial" tunes. We didn't like the songs ourselves, so it's no wonder no one else was buying them. But Dick James just wouldn't change his mind.

This was the period of uncomfortable pressure that Bernie later chronicled in the song "Bitter Fingers," in which he refers to Dick James as one of "those old diehards in Denmark Street." The words to that song refer to the difficulty of writing songs when you have "bitter fingers," but the artwork that accompanies the lyric in the *Captain Fantastic* album doesn't depict a songwriter with bitter fingers. Instead, it depicts a monster wearing a business suit coming across his desk with snakes for fingers. One can't help but notice that this monstrosity bears an eerie resemblance to Dick James. It's a harsh caricature, but what's really amazing is that Elton was still under contract to DJM when the *Captain Fantastic* album was released, so it was Dick James himself who distributed this album!

Nine months went by before Elton John released another single, simply because Dick James refused to approve any of the songs we produced. Time after time I went into his office to play him the tapes of our demos, and time after time he would dismiss one song after another as "not commercial enough." This went on month after month. Reg and Bernie became increasingly frustrated and, after a while, quite understandably, their productivity slowed to a dribble.

While subsequent events proved just how wrong Mr. James was to pursue this course, it is easy to see his motivation for doing so. DJM was and always had been a music publishing house. Dick James made his money by selling sheet music and by selling the rights to songs to various artists. While he was planning to start his own record label, he had not done so yet, so he was less interested in what it would take to make Elton John a star than in what it would take to sell songs to established stars.

My frustration was increased by the fact that we were sacrificing our artistic integrity to produce commercial songs, and we were still being turned down. Anyone who hears these early demos (which have been available on bootleg for several years now) will understand what I mean. There are songs from this period that are clearly Elton John/Bernie Taupin compositions—"Tartan Coloured Lady," "Angel Tree," "When I Was Tealby Abbey," "Regimental Sgt. Zippo," "A Dandelion Dies in the Wind." These songs fit the fantasy-based, drug-drenched sound of that era in popular music, and had Dick James truly been in touch with the times, he would have realized that these were the songs that really would have sold.

But most of the demos we produced during

this period were commercial in the traditional sense —"What the First Tear Shows," "Thank You For All of Your Loving," "You'll Be Sorry to See Me Go," "Where It's At," "There's Still Time for Me." Reg even tried a few more on his own, including "I Get a Little Bit Lonely" and "I Love You and That's All the Matters." We hated doing songs like this, but we did them because Dick James demanded it. And still he was turning us down.

Reg was so distraught that he even tried to get out of his contract with DJM. I took him to see my friend Muff Winwood over at Island Records. Muff is the brother of Steve Winwood, who was then a member of Traffic and who would go on to have a string of solo hits in the early '80s. Muff offered to buy out Reg's contract, but when we presented the offer to Dick James, he turned it down flat. Needless to say, Reg was furious.

The year that had begun with so much promise was turning out to be frustrating for all of us. About the only bright spot took place in the spring, around the release of the first single. Long John Baldry had been nice enough to let Reg open for him at the popular Marquee Club in London. He asked me—along with Dee Murray and Dave Hinds of The Mirage—to back him in his first-ever public appearance as Elton John. We were introduced by the club's owner, Jack Barry. It was an extremely gratifying appearance for Reg, because we basically blew Long John Baldry off the stage!

But when the single went nowhere and Dick

James refused to authorize another, there wasn't much point in pursuing live gigs. Reg and I were both kept busy doing session work for other artists in addition to our work at DJM, but that didn't reduce our frustration. It was the "Summer of Love," and we were all filled with thoughts of freedom and "doing your own thing." Music was about art and self-expression, not about making money. You can imagine how we felt about being held back by someone who was not only a member of the older generation, but who was the epitome of what we called "The Establishment."

Things finally began to change in the fall of 1968, when DJM hired a new promotions man named Steve Brown. Brown was younger and hipper than Stephen James (whose personal musical tastes ran more in the direction of Barbra Streisand than Traffic). Brown had his finger on the pulse of popular music, so he turned out to be essential to the success of DJM's new record label. Brown befriended Reg and Bernie, and when he heard the demos of the songs they loved and compared them to the songs they were being forced to write, he nearly hit the roof. Without the least bit of authority, he told Reg and Bernie to ignore Dick James and write the type of songs they believed in. He also began lobbying Dick and Stephen James to allow the two boys to follow their own hearts.

Brown was just the latest in a series of voices telling Mr. James he was behind the times. Perhaps he was tiring of the fight, because he acquiesced and authorized a second single. I suspect that Brown secured this decision by promising to take full responsibility for the record, because he somehow ended up as its producer, even though he was a promotions man with absolutely no production experience. That was okay, though—whatever it took to move the project forward.

It really didn't matter, anyway, because we were a team that pretty much knew what we were doing. I took care of pulling together the musicians for the session. Brown's real role was mainly that of encourager, and I must say that having a DJM representative who really believed in Reg and Bernie's music was indeed a refreshing change.

The song we had in mind was a haunting, Gothic piece called "Lady Samantha," which would be called a ballad except that it unexpectedly broke into a gallop on the chorus. The song was a wonderful example of the unique sound that Reg and Bernie created together, which means that it didn't fit the commercial mold Mr. James wanted. But even Lionel Conway, head of the firm's publishing division and himself a member of the older generation, argued for its release.

"Lady Samantha" was recorded in October 1968, along with a drug fantasy number called "All Across the Havens" that would serve as the B-side. Because Reg had written the words and music to the first single, these would be the first true Elton John/Bernie Taupin songs ever released by Elton John, and it was my wailing guitar that sounded the opening notes. I also backed him on his first live radio appearance a couple of weeks later, when we played both sides of the single along with "Skyline Pigeon" for the BBC.

About this time, I left Dick James Music to start my own band. One of my assistants, Clive Franks, took over as acting studio manager until a new producer could be found. My friendship with Reg didn't skip a beat, nor did my work on his projects. In November we both played in an impromptu recording band called The Bread and Beer Band, a project put together by another former DJM staffer, Tony King. In December I returned to play guitar on the follow-up single, "It's Me That You Need," and the B-side, "Strange Rain," which wouldn't be released until May 1969. I was back in January to play on the first album, *Empty Sky*.

When "Lady Samantha" came out on

January 17, 1969, it failed to chart and sold fewer than 8,000 copies. However, it received extensive airplay on British radio stations, making it what we in the business call a "turntable hit." The critics were also pleased. *New Musical Express* called it "typically professional and musicianly . . . lyrics are sensible and worthwhile—not part of the underground scene . . . A promising talent." "Elton John's 'Lady Samantha' is nice though it's much as we've heard before," said *Disc & Music Echo*, "Semi-Elizabethan feel but lyrically interesting." Well, it was a lot better reception than the first single had gotten, and it supported our assertion that Reg and Bernie could sell records by writing what came naturally.

Empty Sky was recorded in evening sessions

over about a week's time. It was to be the first album ever released on the new DJM record label.

By that time a fellow named Frank Owen had been hired as studio manager/producer for the new label, so I was surprised to learn that the album was once again going to be produced by Steve Brown. But, again, if that's what it took to get it done, that was fine with me, and it was fine with Reg.

What's ironic about this album is that the songs were even less commercial than many of those that Dick James had previously turned down. It was almost as if, finally freed to chart their own course, Reg and Bernie went a little overboard. No single was released from the album, and although it garnered a few positive (though somewhat mystified) reviews when it was released in June

1969, it quickly disappeared. Dick James ended up with many thousands of copies stuck in his warehouse.

On the one hand, it wasn't a great start for either a new record label or a new artist. On the other hand, Dick and Stephen James were smart to use an unknown artist in their own stable for their first recording project, giving them time to work out the kinks and learn the inevitable lessons of a new venture. Stephen James knew his record label wasn't ready to host a big name, and Elton John needed just a little more time to "get his act together" (literally), so it was really a mutually beneficial situation.

Regarding the content of the album, my theory is that we were witnessing a step in the long process of Reg and Bernie refining their style, a process that I believe had been delayed by Dick James's insistence that they write popular songs. *Empty Sky* is the juvenilia that should have been produced by Elton John and Bernie Taupin the year before, so that by 1969 they would have learned to temper the mysticism and obscurity of the lyrics and to bring a fuller sound to the music. Instead, this process had been lengthened by a year. The proof of this lies in the album they wrote and recorded one year later.

I spent the remainder of 1969 putting together and playing with my own band. In January 1970, I was called in to play on Elton's second album, to be called simply *Elton John*. To make sure they did it right this time, Steve Brown brought on board Gus Dudgeon and Paul Buckmaster, the producer and arranger for David Bowie's recent hit "Space Oddity." They, in turn, brought in a variety of very professional session musicians, including a string section. Steve also booked Trident Studios for the new album, which meant we were recording with sixteen tracks instead of four.

It's obvious that Dudgeon and Buckmaster actually took the time to listen to the songs—and even read the lyrics—prior to starting the sessions. How else could they have so perfectly matched the mood of those songs? Buckmaster didn't just add strings to the arrangements; he actually charted the music from the rhythm section out, so everything worked together as a seamless whole. (Elton later departed from this approach, and I believe his music suffered as a result.) On this project I was truly just a session musician, brought in to play on only four tracks, but I remember that when I arrived at the studio, we all knew exactly what we were going to do, and that was thanks to Gus and Paul.

A few days before the album sessions were to begin, I received a call from Reg asking me to come around to his mum's flat next time I was in London. A day or two later I dropped by, and he played for me a gospel-infused song called "Border Song," which I loved immediately. It ended with the lines, "There's a man over there. What's his color? I don't care. He's my brother; let us live in peace." And just before he sang those lines, he looked at me and said, "This is for you." It turned out that Reg had written those lines because the lyric given to him by Bernie had been too short. In the years since, some have criticized those lines as being trite, but, needless to say, they mean a lot to me.

The *Elton John* sessions were much more professional than those for *Empty Sky*. They were much more organized, with Paul Buckmaster having actually composed the lead guitar part to play in unison with the strings in some places, something that I had never seen done before. The sessions were also much more fun, because it turned out that Gus Dudgeon shared Reg's zany sense of humor. I remember laughing quite a bit during those sessions.

As I mentioned earlier, Reg and I had long been working to blend the sounds of guitar and piano, and I think this effort came to fruition on the *Elton John* album. You can hear it on almost every track, including those that I didn't play on. It's easy to hear on the softer songs such as "Your Song" and "First Episode at Hienton," but it's equally true on the rock songs such as "Take Me to the Pilot." All those long hours of work finally paid off in this album, and everything we had been working to develop came together for the first time.

In addition to "Take Me to the Pilot" and "The Cage," I played on "No Shoestrings on Louise," a conscious effort to copy The Rolling Stones. We had already copied The Stones on the title track to *Empty Sky*, which we had specifically discussed as a "Gimme Shelter"-type song. In the middle of "Empty Sky," we even inserted a long instrumental interlude with hushing vocals that was copped from The Stones' "Going Home" from their 1966 *Aftermath* album. Musically, "No Shoestrings on Louise" paid homage to the country influence of a lot of Stones songs, using a three-quarter time with the emphasis on the first beat. If you listen to Elton's vocal, you can tell he's trying to be Mick Jagger on that song.

I also played acoustic guitar on "First Episode at Hienton." To me, that song is classic early Elton John, for several reasons. Musically, there is that perfect blend of piano and guitar that we had worked so hard to achieve. Lyrically, there is an English classicism, with a wide-open landscape about it. The song breathes, with its strong poetic images matched by its strong musical images. The song is not stuffy or heavy, but is instead very free. That's the beauty of that early stuff.

Also on that album was a sweet little ballad called "Your Song." I'm speaking the absolute truth when I say that no one involved in the project considered that song to be a candidate for a single. We thought it was a nice song, but we were all focused more on the harder-edged songs—the rock influence of "Take Me to the Pilot," the country influence of "No Shoestrings on Louise," the gospel influence of "Border Song." If you listen to the piano-only demo of "Your Song," you'll notice that it comes across a little too soft and mushy—sort of like a Carpenters song—which was not a sound that was going to impress us. In fact, in the final recording, "Your Song" is saved from sounding too soft only by the light R&B drumbeat that Barry Morgan puts under it. In any case, none of us saw the song as a standout.

Elton John was released in England in April 1970 and in America in June, but sales were slow in both countries. "Border Song" was the first single to be released from the album, but it bombed in England and stalled at number ninety-two on the American charts. Counting his work with Bluesology, this was Reg's sixth single to be released and his sixth single to fail to make the British charts. On the American front, DJM's usual American licensee had turned Elton John down, and he ended up being released on the Uni label, a small subsidiary of MCA Records. Obviously, no one held out much hope of anything happening over there.

The only encouraging thing that happened in the early months after the album's release was that Aretha Franklin decided to do a version of "Border Song." Needless to say, we were huge fans of Aretha, following her amazing commercial success of the prior three years, which included a string of Top Ten hits like "Think," "Respect," "Chain of Fools," and "Natural Woman." Reg and Bernie were thrilled that she was going to cover one of their songs, and when the import single came in, I got a call to come to his mum's house to hear "Border Song" once again, this time in Aretha's voice emanating from the little 45 rpm record with the red-and-black Atlantic label. We were all happy when the song climbed to number thirty-seven on the American pop charts, giving the songwriting team of Elton John and Bernie Taupin their first Top Forty hit in any country. But that still didn't help Elton John the artist, whose album continued to languish on both sides of the Atlantic.

Meanwhile, Reg had put together his own band. He wanted his piano to be the focal point on stage, so he added only a rhythm section—a drummer and a bass player. The bass player was our old friend Dee Murray of The Mirage, who had played on the early demos, and the drummer was Nigel Olsson, the former lead vocalist for Plastic Penny. Both The Mirage and Plastic Penny had been DJM groups. The new group had started playing their first club dates in the fall of 1969, with

Steve Brown providing management services for the time being.

It turned out that the folks at Uni Records really liked the *Elton John* album, and they were willing to put their marketing resources behind it if Elton would come over to play live as part of the effort. The record company got him booked for week-long engagements at The Troubadour clubs in Los Angeles and San Francisco, the preeminent showcases of new talent at that time. The catch was that the gig paid only about $500, leaving Dick James to underwrite the expense of sending the band to America. Dick was willing to do it, but I distinctly remember the feeling among all of us that this was a last-ditch effort to get Elton John launched. We'd tried everything—released a bunch of singles, made two albums—and nothing was working. Dick still believed in Reg, but the feeling remained that a failure in America would mean that we were getting close to the time for some serious reconsideration.

Even Reg wasn't keen on going. He didn't think that playing a couple of club dates was going to make any difference, and he kept saying that he didn't think the new band was ready yet. At the same time, what young man in England could turn down a free trip to America? Bernie was certainly keen to see the land he had loved from afar since childhood. In the end, the trip was arranged, and in August 1970 the group flew off without fanfare and in coach-fare seats.

By this time, my new band, Hookfoot, had

gotten a contract with Dick James Music. We were in the studio recording our first album when Steve Brown returned from America. "You're not going to be believe this," he said. "Elton John is the biggest thing going in Los Angeles. Leon Russell and all the big names are showing up. They got Neil Diamond to introduce him! The music reviewer for the *Los Angeles Times* loves him. Reg is doing all this Jerry Lee Lewis stuff, kicking away his piano stool and doing handstands on the keyboard."

"Reg???" we all asked incredulously.

"Yes," Brown went on. "He's coming out wearing shorts and boots with wings painted on them." We were amazed. We all knew that Reg was capable of outbursts of outrageous behavior, but, except for those days with Bluesology when he stalked around the stage destroying equipment, we had never seen him act the least bit energetic on stage. But Brown told us that Reg was still in America because additional gigs had popped up as a result of the enormous buzz he was creating.

When he got back, the first time I saw him was in the office. I remember him very enthusiastically telling me all about it. He was still the quiet and humble Reg, but when he talked about the American performances, his eyes shone with a new light.

Almost immediately, Elton had to go back to America with Dee and Nigel for some further appearances generated by the excitement of the first visit. Uni Records wanted a second single to coincide with the visit, so they released "Your Song," which we considered to be an odd selection. The last thing Elton John needed was another single that didn't chart. As proof of our lack of faith in that song's potential, the second single to be released in England was "Take Me To The Pilot," with "Your Song" as the B-side.

The next thing we knew, Elton John had cracked America. In October, the *Elton John* album entered the Top Forty, then rose to number four. In December, "Your Song" entered the Top Forty, where it rose to number eight. The album went gold and stayed in the American Top Forty for twenty-eight weeks. *Tumbleweed Connection*, released in January 1971, climbed to number five, stayed in the Top Forty for twenty weeks, and went gold in two months, all without the benefit of a single. The soundtrack to *Friends*, released in March, went gold in one month. *11-17-70*, a live album recorded during Elton's second U.S. visit and released in May, gave Elton his fourth consecutive Top Forty album, all in a period of only seven months.

After all the years of struggle, he was, quite literally, an overnight success in the States. During his second trip, he received the highest amount ever paid to a first-time artist appearing at the Fillmore East. Bob Dylan came backstage to meet him and Bernie and publicly praised them. As soon as Elton came home, he had to turn right around and go back for a legitimate tour of larger venues. The success of "Your Song" in America caused Dick James to release it in England in January 1971, and it rose to number seven, giving Elton and Bernie a Top Ten hit on both sides of the Atlantic.

We were surprised by the suddenness of it all, Elton included. In just a matter of months, he went from total anonymity to not being able to walk down the street. What was even stranger, England didn't catch on the way America did, so he could be mobbed at the airport as he left America and then walk down the corridor at Gatwick without anyone noticing him. All the top stars were suddenly praising Elton John, and we were all left shaking our heads in bemusement. "My goodness, what's going on here?" we wondered.

The funniest thing to us—and, again, to Elton himself—was the idea that shy, stocky, goofy, and prematurely balding Reg Dwight was suddenly being looked at by thousands of young girls as a sex symbol. I mean, we didn't think of him in Bunter terms by then, but we certainly didn't see him as a sex symbol!

In June 1971, we went back into the studio to record his next album, entitled *Madman Across the Water*. Released in November 1971, the album went gold in three months. From that point on, he could do no wrong, especially in America. *Honky Chateau*, released in May 1972, went gold in two months, spawned two Top Ten hits, and became Elton's first number-one album. It turned out to be the first of six consecutive number-one studio albums. *Don't Shoot Me, I'm Only the Piano Player*, released in January 1973, went gold in three weeks and produced a number-one and a number-two hit. Then came the *coup de grace.*

In October 1973, Elton released a double album entitled *Goodbye, Yellow Brick Road.* Even though it was a more expensive double album, it went gold in America in seven days. Like the previous album, it rose to number one in both America and England, and it stayed at the top of the American charts for eight weeks. It would remain in the American Top Forty for forty-three weeks and in the Billboard Top 200 for—are you ready for this?—four and a half years. It spawned three Top Twenty hits in both America and England. In America, this included "Bennie and the Jets," which rose to number one on the pop charts and crossed over to reach number fifteen on the R&B charts.

By this time, Elton was famous for his over-the-top stage costumes and his legendary collection of wild glasses. He was, like Elvis and The Beatles before him and Michael Jackson and Madonna after him, becoming a cultural phenomenon that transcended the world of popular music.

To get an idea of how quickly all this happened, just look at the singles Elton released, all of them considered pop music classics today. From November 1971 to October 1973—a period of exactly two years—he released "Tiny Dancer," "Levon," "Honky Cat," "Rocket Man," "Crocodile Rock," "Daniel," "Saturday Night's Alright for Fighting," "Goodbye, Yellow Brick Road," "Candle in the Wind" (in England only) and "Bennie and the Jets" (in America only). That's a hit almost every other month! Two of these songs hit number one on the American charts; two others hit number two. All but two made the Top Twenty, and only "Tiny Dancer" missed the Top Forty, stalling at number forty-one.

For the most part, these are the songs that would appear on Elton's first greatest hits collection in 1974, which shipped gold and went platinum by the end of the year. The best-selling album of 1975, it was the first greatest hits collection to enter the British charts at number one and the first to reach the top of the American charts by its second week. It remained the number-one album in America for ten weeks and in the Billboard Top 200 for exactly two years. Today, the album has sold more than seventeen million copies in America alone, making it one of the best-selling greatest hits collections of all time.

Naturally, things changed rapidly for Elton on a personal level, as well. He had four consecutive Top Forty albums in America while still living in his mum's flat in Pinner. Two and a half years later, with the release of *Goodbye Yellow Brick Road*, he was undeniably the greatest superstar in the world and the biggest thing to happen to popular music since The Beatles.

Back in 1971, even with his early success in America, we never would have dreamed how far it would go. What we did see was a young man whose shyness was finally disappearing and whose personality was starting to emerge. We were about to find out—the whole world was about to find out

—just how much this young man had bottled up from his repressed childhood.

In December of that year, my band, Hookfoot, was working on our second album when Steve Brown once again dropped by the studio.

"You're not going to believe this," he said. "Reg is really Elton now. He went down and changed his name by deed poll."

"What?" we all said in unison. "You've got to be kidding."

"Not just that," Steve said. "He's added a middle name. His full legal name is now Elton Hercules John." Well, we were all beside ourselves. After it sank in that Reg had really done this, I remember thinking how ridiculous the whole thing was. I mean, "Hercules"? Where had that come

177

from? It was one of the first little hints to me that Elton and I, as close as we were, had very different lives to lead.

Chapter Six

Hookfoot

When I was working on Denmark Street in the 1960s, there arose among people of my age a great interest in Eastern religion and Transcendental Meditation. This was especially true for those of us in the music business, inspired as we were by The Beatles and their association with the Maharishi Mahesh Yogi. And there I was, a teenager who had been abandoned by his father, who had seen his mother crack up, who was filled with pain and didn't know what to do with it. Like anyone in such a situation, I was searching for God, but I didn't know where to start.

I couldn't just go to church, because that was

what our parents' generation did, and the most important thing to my generation was to reject everything our parents held dear. After all, we would tell each other, the Christian church has caused much of the pain in the world, from the Spanish Inquisition to the Salem Witch Trials, and it supported such atrocities as slavery. Even if you didn't count all that, 2,000 years of Christianity had failed to cure the poverty and sickness and tyranny in the world, so what good was it? We were looking for something new.

Ironically, what we turned to was even older than Christianity. I read everything I could on the occult and on Eastern religions. I spent hours browsing through bookstores looking for dusty texts that seemed mystical just because they were old. I took part in all-night "rap" sessions in which we discussed the mysteries of the universe while smoking pot. I even joined a meditation group at a place called the School of Meditation.

I became particularly attracted to Buddhism, and one day when I was nineteen, I made up my mind that I was going to become a Buddhist. I took a train to Hampstead, which is just outside London, and I went to this Buddhist temple and knocked on the door. The door opened and this very peculiar person—who was dressed in an orange robe and who had no hair—asked me to come in. I walked in and looked around at all this weird stuff on the walls.

"What can we do for you?" the guy said.

"I'm thinking about becoming a Buddhist," I

said. You could tell by the expression on his face that he was skeptical—I'm sure in those days I must have been one in a long line of stoned hippies coming to the door seeking to do the cool thing of the moment. He invited me in and started telling me about the steps I would have to take, but he obviously thought that I would back out once I learned that there was actual work involved.

"You'll have to study the five precepts," he said.

"I've already read them," I said. His eyes widened a bit, and his expression began to change. As he learned how much I already knew, he began to think that he had found a new recruit. But, oddly, the more confident he became, the more uncertain I became. Then, all of a sudden, deep down inside of me, a voice said, "No." Just "No." I turned around and walked out the door.

Still, I kept searching for something supernatural in my life. I knew a lot of people who embraced Satan worship, and while I never tinkered with it myself, I did listen with interest to those who did. For example, I knew a man in London, who was in his late fifties at the time, who in his younger days had been a student of a man named Alister Crowley, the leader of satanic circles in Europe. Later, Jimmy Page of Led Zeppelin bought Crowley's house and lived there. But I knew that wasn't for me.

In the meantime, I used drugs to numb my underlying sense of incompleteness. Voltaire said that all of us have a "God-shaped void" in our lives, and for years I tried to fill that void by shoveling drugs into it. But after the drugs wore off, it seemed as if the void was bigger than before, and the only answer was to take more drugs. That was no problem, because everyone else I knew was doing the same thing. The fact that my career was going well also made it easy to ignore the pain.

Back in 1965, when I had first joined DJM, my sister Terri was working for the management of R&B singer Georgie Fame. Georgie was scheduled to appear on the BBC television show *Ready, Steady, Go!*, and Terri was nice enough to get me tickets. Also on the show that day was the brilliant blues guitarist Buddy Guy, and he was backed by a band from Southampton called The Soul Agents. The Soul Agents were a jazz/R&B trio made up of an organist, a drummer, and a bass player.

Under normal circumstances, I wouldn't have noticed the band, because back then on television shows like *Ready, Steady, Go!*, the bands usually came on and lip-synced their own records. The studio audience didn't actually get to see them play, so there would be no way of knowing how good they really were. But on this particular occasion, the BBC was preparing to take the show live, and they wanted to do a few test runs before they did so. As a result, I got to see The Soul Agents actually play, and I was impressed.

I noticed especially their drummer, Roger Pope. He had a very solid swing, very solid time. His backbeat impressed me because it reminded me of Art Blakey, and at that time there were very few

English drummers who could play like that. Back in those days, most English drummers were pretty messy. The Soul Agents did three numbers with Buddy Guy, and by the time it was over, the band had my respect.

One of the top producers of the day was Larry Page, whose company Page One Records was partially owned by Dick James Music. As a result, I often produced demos and did session work for Larry. He was the producer of The Troggs, which is how I ended up playing guitar on many of their records. Soon after I first saw The Soul Agents, they came in to audition for Larry, with me serving as recording engineer. The group had a great organist in Don Shinn, and the music they did was sort of jazz/blues with a strong, driving groove. I still liked them, but apparently they weren't what Larry was looking for, because they failed to get a recording contract. Soon after that, Don Shinn came down with tuberculosis, and the band fell apart.

I wasn't the only one impressed with Roger Pope's drumming, because I soon heard that Ronnie Bond, the drummer for The Troggs, had asked Roger to teach him some of his techniques. Roger ended up going with the band on their American tour, where they were opening for The Who, as a drum tutor and roadie. After he got back, he rejoined Dave Glover, bassist for The Soul Agents, and they formed a new band called The Loot. The Loot, unlike The Soul Agents, did land a recording contract with Page One Records, and it wasn't long before I was brought in to play on one of their first records. Unfortunately, The Loot never really got off the ground, and by the fall of 1968, it had all but fallen apart.

One day I ran into Dave Glover—whom everyone called "Gloves"—at DJM. I told him I needed a rhythm section for a session for a guy named Reg Dwight, and I asked him if he and Roger would be interested. Roger and Gloves came in to record the "Lady Samantha" single and its B-side, and all of us, Elton included, liked what we heard. During the breaks, Roger and I started jamming together, and it was immediately apparent that we shared the same musical tastes.

Before the night was over, Roger was telling me that we needed to form our own band. I resisted at first, telling him that I was really hitting my stride on the session work around town. But he insisted, and he made me promise to come with him to Andover to meet his manager, Stan Phillips. When I went with him several days later, I was impressed to find that Phillips was a manager who believed in backing his groups financially. When Roger, Gloves, and I jammed together in Andover, it certainly confirmed that we were all headed in the same musical direction. A couple of weeks later, when Elton played "Lady Samantha" on BBC Radio, it was me, Roger, and Gloves that backed him.

    Just at that time, The Loot, which was basically defunct, suddenly found that it had a minor hit with a song called "She's A Winner."

They needed another guitar player to support their subsequent club appearances, so they asked me to join. The band fell apart again almost immediately, but by that time I was fully on board with the idea of forming a band with Roger and Dave. When I resigned from Dick James Music toward the end of 1968, it was with the intention of putting all my effort into starting this band.

Roger brought on board a friend named Ian Duck, who was a blues harmonica player, and our quartet was complete. The reason Roger and Dave had moved to Andover—a town about thirty miles north of their hometown of Southampton and about an hour and a half outside London—is that it was the headquarters of Stan Phillips's operations. I moved out of my mum's house and joined them. I would still drive my green Hillman Californian into London to do session work or to go out on the weekends, so this was in no way an attempt to divorce ourselves from the London music scene. We just wanted to get far enough away to devote our full energies to developing our sound.

We played a lot of local gigs in towns in the area. We practiced every day and played every night we could find an audience. We practiced in a small village hall called Clanville Hall, for which we had to pay a small weekly fee. It was a dirty, one-room, unheated place out in the middle of nowhere, and we four long-haired hippie types were, I'm sure, the talk of the local villagers.

The floor of Clanville Hall was wooden, and when we played, Roger Pope's drums would start moving around on him. His highhat, being so light, was especially troublesome, so he figured out a way to hook his foot around it to keep it from sliding away. Perhaps the pot and the booze made this seem funnier than it was, but the end result was that we named our band Hookfoot.

The members of Hookfoot all eschewed mainstream pop music, and none more so than myself. I considered myself a serious musician—partially because of my family heritage—and I had been heavily influenced by my recent live exposure to Jimi Hendrix. I was getting very much into the funky, R&B-influenced music that was becoming all the rage in the underground, and as the lead guitarist and the main songwriter, I took the band in that direction. We were one of the first bands to fuse R&B and rock, so the reviewers often referred to us as a "funk/fusion" band. Unfortunately, this meant we didn't fit neatly into any category of popular music, and funk music had not come into its own at that time. The simple fact is that we were ahead of our time.

When Hookfoot first started, Elton didn't have his own band, so we backed him on just about every project. We joined him in the impromptu Bread and Beer Band that released a single of "The Dick Barton Theme." In December, we were back in the studio with him to record his follow-up single, "It's Me That You Need." Roger and I were back in January to work on the *Empty Sky* album. Hookfoot also backed him on a couple more appearances on the BBC.

During this time, and all the way through the following spring, Elton would come to our practice sessions and work out his songs with us. He would also come to some of our club gigs and try his songs out on our audiences. I remember specifically that we helped him work out "Empty Sky," "Lady, What's Tomorrow," and "Sails" prior to helping him record them for the *Empty Sky* album. When it came time to record the *Elton John* album a year later, I played on "Take Me to the Pilot" and "The Cage" because I had already been playing them live with Elton. I also remember helping him premiere "Ballad of a Well-Known Gun" and "Son of Your Father" several months before we recorded them for the *Tumbleweed Connection* album in the fall of 1970.

In the spring of 1969, after Hookfoot had gotten a good number of songs under our belts, we went down to London to record some demos. We recorded our first set—about twelve songs—at PYE Studios. About that time, word went out that Marshall Chess of Chess Records—the very famous R&B label in Chicago—was coming to England to look for new acts. We were huge fans of Chess. Stan Phillips, our manager, pulled the right strings and presented our demos to Marshall. Lo and behold, we landed a contract with Chess Records based on our first demos.

We couldn't have been more thrilled. We knew for sure that we were on our way. We went into PYE Studios and recorded our first album, then turned the tapes over to Marshall to take back to

America for mixing. We were confident that the album would be mixed with that wonderful blues sound for which Chess was so admired.

Six months went by without a word. Finally, Geoffrey Heath, at our music publisher's office in London, called us and told us the tapes of the final mix had come in. We went up to London and sat down in Heath's office, all of us excited about hearing our first album. But when Geoffrey turned on the tape, our spirits fell. It sounded terrible. They had edited all sorts of stuff and given the whole thing a very thin sound. The longer it played, the more agitated we became.

"That album is not going out," I said firmly. Poor Geoffery was caught in the middle. On the one hand, he knew that we had a contract that required us to support the album with live appearances and that we didn't have the legal right to prevent the album from coming out. On the other hand, he had no authority to take action if we really did decide to revolt. Besides, this probably wasn't the first time he had seen a band disappointed with a first hearing of an album. He probably thought we would calm down after a while.

He didn't know who he was dealing with. We took our music, and our reputations as musicians, very seriously. The release of an album like this would destroy what we had spent every waking moment of the last year trying to build. We went back to Andover and began to scheme on how we could get out of this miserable contract.

The next week, the members of Hookfoot

once again showed up at the office of Geoffrey Heath, Esq. We acted disappointed when the secretary told us he wasn't in. Little did she know that we had arranged our visit because we knew he was out of town. Roger Pope and I struck up a conversation with the secretary, and as we chatted her up, Dave Glover sidled around behind her and slipped in to Geoffrey's office. He quickly found our contract in Geoffrey's files and stuck it under his shirt. When he slipped back out of the door, Roger and I could tell by his smile that he had succeeded.

"Well, tell Geoffrey we just dropped by to say hello," we said cheerfully as we backed out of the door. The secretary assured us with a smile that she would. As far as we know, she didn't hear the schoolboy whoops of joy we let out once we got out onto the street. The contract went to Stan Phillips, Stan called Chess and told them they had no contract, and that was the end of our disappointing tenure with Chess Records.

Despite our dramatic little coup in stealing the contract, the whole experience was a real kick in the guts after the excitement of thinking we were on our way. Still, we were being received well in our club appearances, and by 1970 we were being booked into the larger London clubs. The most famous club was The Flamingo, and herein lies a story that shows how small the world is.

Elton had played at The Flamingo with Bluesology both before and after the addition of Long John Baldry. In 1967, my mother had gotten remarried to a very nice man named Harry Gunnell (who is now deceased). Harry worked in a shipping insurance firm called Crumps and had been a longtime friend of the family. He had two sons named Rik and John Gunnell, who were quite a bit older than me. Rik and John were impresarios in the music industry. They were the owners of The Flamingo and had been the managers of Long John Baldry even before he joined Bluesology. This meant that Elton's band was being managed, quite coincidentally, by my brothers-in-law! That family connection had nothing to do with either Bluesology or Hookfoot getting to play at The Flamingo—we were both established bands with legitimate followings—but I remember thinking even then what a coincidence it all was.

The members of Hookfoot were somewhat frustrated about not having a recording contract, but we were so busy that we didn't have much time to worry about it. In addition to writing and recording our own songs and playing live gigs, we were much in demand as a session band for other groups' albums. We backed American acts on their British and European tours, including Al Kooper, founder of Blood Sweat & Tears. We were also becoming very popular on the college circuit. Pretty soon we had a solid reputation as the top band on the underground circuit. We were a band that you had to be cool to even know about, and one that you had to know about in order to be cool.

In March 1970, we returned to Trident Studios to record Elton's third album, *Tumbleweed*

Connection. The lyrics Bernie Taupin handed to Elton for this album were all about the American Old West, inspired by Bernie's longtime fascination with that subject and by the recent music of The Band. The *Elton John* album had taken some critical hits for its "over-instrumentation," so Elton and Gus made a conscious decision to create an earthier, rawer sound for the new album. You couldn't get any earthier or rawer than Hookfoot, and there we were playing on various DJM projects, so we were recruited *en masse* as the main studio band for the album. As a result, Dee and Nigel, who had only been Elton's backing band for several months, ended up playing on only one track, "Amoreena," and then only because they had been playing it live.

It's often been noted that *Tumbleweed Connection* is unlike any other Elton John album. Hookfoot is the reason. Because of his training at the Royal Academy of Music, Elton has always composed tightly structured tunes based on classical piano chords. On this project, we came in and laid down a blanket of pure, unadulterated funk on top of those chords. I was given the freedom to let loose on my guitar in a way that I wasn't on the earlier projects, and you can tell with my opening notes that this will not be an album that will put anyone to sleep. I was pleased to hear that Gus Dudgeon once said Elton could never have made an album like *Tumbleweed Connection* without Hookfoot.

It you want to get an idea of what Hookfoot

was like in comparison to Elton and other bands, just look at our photos in the lyric booklet of the original album release. Everyone had long hair back then, of course, but if you'll look at me and my bandmates, you'll see what a rough and rustic bunch we were. (Those photos were taken on the roof of Dick James Music, and I think you can tell that I was in a really foul mood, because we had just come off the road and needed a rest, but they insisted on taking the photos that day.) If we look to you like a bunch of hippie dope fiends, well, we were.

Soon after the *Elton John* album was released in April 1970, Hookfoot signed a recording contract with Dick James Music. Now my friend Reg and I both had recording contracts, and they were with the same record label. We couldn't have been happier. My attention became focused on writing and recording our first album for release in 1971. That's why we were in the DJM studio when word came back that Elton was wowing the celebrity-studded audience at the Troubadour.

Just before Elton went to America, we put the finishing touches on his next album, *Madman Across the Water*. Hookfoot played on three cuts —"Tiny Dancer," "Razor Face," and "Holiday Inn"—and I also played on "Levon." Despite our presence, this album was anything but *Elton John Meets Hookfoot, Part II*. I'm not sure what happened on this project, but the fears about "over-instrumentation" must have been set aside, because this album ended up even heavier than the *Elton*

John album. It certainly contains some classic tracks and is nothing to be ashamed of, but I agree with some of the music critics who considered it to be somewhat of a step backwards.

In early 1971, just as Elton was finding stardom in America, Hookfoot was launched. Our self-titled first album was released and we appeared live on the BBC. The record company set us up on tours of England, Europe, and Scandinavia. We played at the rock festivals that were so popular after Woodstock, sometimes to crowds as large as 500,000 (some of whom were actually listening to the music!). A&M Records brought us to the States, where we opened for such performers as Jefferson Airplane, Paul Butterfield, Boz Scaggs, and, on a few occasions in those early months,

Elton John. Over the next three years, Hookfoot released four albums, all of them critical, though not commercial, successes.

I've often been asked if I regretted not being a part of Elton's success, or if I was jealous of it, but nothing could be further from the truth. First of all, his success was the fulfillment of a project we had been working on for several years, and I felt a great deal of pride in having been instrumental in launching that career. Second, as you can see, I had my own thing going during those early years, and it was going very well. I had formed Hookfoot before Elton cut his first album, and the reason I wasn't in his band was not because he didn't want me, but because I wasn't available. Of course, Hookfoot wasn't the phenomenon that Elton was, but few are.

I was playing the kind of music I liked, getting positive critical reviews, enjoying a strong underground following, and making excellent money. I had absolutely no reason to be jealous of my friend.

While Hookfoot's first appearance on BBC radio was backing Elton, we later made appearances on our own. Playing the BBC was always an experience because the organization was so stodgy. The studio was in a very old, ornate building called Aeolian Hall, with uniformed doormen standing outside. The BBC was very unionized, and the guys engineering the shows were older guys who were used to recording dance bands, not rock bands. They didn't try to hide their disdain for us hippie types. The Saturday afternoon pop shows were played live, and the technology was laughable by today's standards. They would just put old ribbon microphones in front of the vocalists and the amplifier speakers, and when the red light came on, you began. There would be a live audience of a couple of hundred teenyboppers who screamed a lot, because that's what you were supposed to do in those post-Beatles days.

We also appeared on BBC television. I remember one show in particular called *Disco 2*. The host was this hippie named John Peel, a deejay whose radio show was called *The Perfume Garden*, a title that pretty much explained where he was coming from. Hookfoot backed several acts on *Disco 2*, including Seals & Crofts with their big 1972 hit "Summer Breeze," Billy Preston (before

"Will It Go Round in Circles"), and others. Throughout all this, my session work continued. For example, I remember playing on Lou Reed's first solo album after he left the Velvet Underground in 1972.

It was with the success of Hookfoot that sin entered my life in a major way. The drugs and sex had already been there, but now they were about to become, for lack of a better word, institutionalized in my life. With the money and the contacts would come unlimited access to drugs. With fame would come unlimited access to women. By that time I was already dating the woman who would become my first wife, but I'm ashamed to say that that had no effect on my "recreational activities" while on the road. This was, after all, the age of "free love."

The band members weren't the only ones practicing free love. At the music festivals where we would play, the crowd would be taking drugs, making out, and sometimes even having sex under their blankets in the grass or mud. (Remember, this was England, so the majority of these outdoor festivals would be rained on. It could get pretty messy.) Oftentimes we would see women going topless, and even more often women near the stage would flash us by lifting or opening their shirts. This didn't just happen at the love festivals, either. Throughout my career in rock & roll, in both outdoor and indoor venues, I would see women flashing us from the floor, or getting up on their boyfriend's shoulders and taking off their tops for several songs, or for as long as they could without the security guards doing something about it.

When Hookfoot first started out, it was still mostly a matter of easy pickups where women were concerned. But after we released our first album, the record company put us on tour and gave us an entourage that included two roadies. Now, the job of a roadie is to take care of whatever the band needs, and that includes acting as a gatekeeper for women, if not for drugs. Playing behind Long John Baldry in a cabaret club, you could walk out on the floor after the show without being mobbed. But once your picture is on the cover of an album, such easy audience contact is foolhardy, and you become a prisoner of the backstage, the limousine, and the hotel room. That leaves the roadie as your guard, and a standing instruction to any roadie is to allow in—or track down and invite in—the most willing and beautiful women in the audience.

When that first record tour started and we realized that we now had guys who could bring us women after every show, we felt a strange mixture of emotions. On the one hand, we had been around rock & roll long enough to be pretty sophisticated, and we certainly didn't want to act surprised or anything. On the other hand, we did kind of feel like kids in a candy store. The first couple of times, we couldn't help but smile at each other and say, "Well, boys, we have arrived."

I remember in particular a tour of Italy in 1971. There were women throwing themselves at us on that one. Most of these women couldn't even speak English, and we couldn't speak a word of

Italian. (In fact, with all the drugs and drinking, we could barely speak English ourselves.) So there was nothing but a lot of sign language or, to be more exact, a lot of body language. Women would always get backstage—some because they had backstage passes, some because they had just charmed the roadies, and some because the roadies had invited them. You could tell which women were just starry-eyed fans and which were interested in a more intimate relationship. We'd take them back to the hotel with us in the limousine. When we got back to the hotel, there would be food and drinks and drugs, and then we'd pair off and go to our rooms and have sex. It was as simple as that, show after show after show.

    Many times the women would know where

we could get drugs, and it wasn't long before we had a network all across Britain and the Continent to supply our needs whenever we passed through town. By that time, my recreational use of marijuana had turned into a hardcore drug habit involving just about everything available.

In 1970, before we had even released our first album, we went to Finland to play in the Helsinki Pop Festival. Three groups were sent over together as sort of ambassadors from the British music scene—Hookfoot, a band called Fairport Convention (which is still going today), and a solo act named Edgar Broughton, who had a cult hit called "Out, Demons, Out." Broughton was a big, hairy, hippie-looking guy who played guitar. We were all in this chartered plane with our roadies and entourages, and I had never seen so many drugs in all my life. We just partied our way across the North Sea. But when we landed at Helsinki Airport and began taxiing down the runway, we looked out the window and saw a whole line of armored police vehicles and a large group of uniformed policemen waiting for us out on the tarmac. They knew that several rock bands were coming in on this plane, so they figured they had an easy bust. As we drew closer, we could see their machine guns and drug dogs.

Needless to say, the party turned into panic. Everyone started eating their drugs, myself included. Remember, we were already high, so our bloodstreams already contained more drugs than was safe, yet here were people eating cocaine and popping pills as fast as they could. I thought I was bad off because I had a block of hash, but Edgar Broughton was eating tabs of LSD as well as other things.

They took us into the terminal and searched us while the dogs searched the plane. Amazingly, they didn't find a thing! We were set free, even though we were so high that most of us were starting to feel sick. We loaded all our equipment onto the double-decker bus that was to take us to the festival and piled in. I remember that the fellow driving the bus was very old, and just as he was turning into the stadium entrance, he turned the bus over on its side in a ditch beside the road. So here are all these stoned rock musicians climbing out of the windows of this bus, pulling their equipment out, screaming bloody murder at this poor old Finnish bus driver who probably couldn't understand a word of English (although I'm sure he got the gist of what they were saying). We had to carry all our equipment all the way across the huge stadium parking lot, which was no easy task because all those drugs we had eaten were starting to take effect. And we still had to set up and play. It was a nightmare.

Edgar Broughton was up first, and he'd eaten all this LSD, so when he started playing his guitar, it was the most horrendous playing I had ever heard. Now, in my humble opinion, Broughton wasn't much of a guitar player to begin with, but that night it was extra special. He hadn't even bothered to tune his guitar before starting. The crowd—who were also mostly high—started cheering, but I was just cracking up. The hash I had eaten had started to kick in, so I was feeling fine. I was standing next to David Peg, the bass player for Fairport Convention. I turned to him and said in a very serious voice, "So, Dave, what do you think?" With a perfectly straight face, he said, "The songs are okay, but the arrangements need a little work." I was screaming in hysterics.

After he had played his big cult hit, "Out, Demons, Out," Broughton came off stage and proceeded to throw up for an extended period of time. The joke for the rest of the trip was "Out, Tomato Skins, Out," or whatever other kind of food we decided to use to fill in the blank.

Well, the whole festival had to be shut down

by the police at about 2:00 am, because it turned out that two guys—yes, two males—had been raped and murdered there on the grounds.

I wasn't able to discern Satan's presence back then, but as I look back on it now, I know that he was there. Ironically, those of us in the hippie generation thought we were going to change the world through "free love" and the "heightened awareness" made possible by drug use. Somehow, we honestly convinced ourselves that we could make a better world by getting stoned and having sex whenever we wanted. In retrospect, it was a pretty blatant case of people trying to justify their behavior, but during that time we really believed we were forging a better way.

Many of my fellow members of that

generation like to complain that our movement lost out to the hedonism of the '70s, but they're just kidding themselves. The "Me Decade" of the '70s was a direct result of the habits we formed in the '60s. The '60s were all about hedonism—sex, drugs, abandoning moral values, dropping out of society, not working. The hedonism of the '70s was an extension of the cultural values of the hippies, not a departure from it. By the late '70s, the '60s slogan of "peace and love" had given way to the battle cry of "Sex, Drugs, and Rock 'n' Roll!", and what list could better describe the youth culture of the '60s? As least in the '70s they weren't trying to fool themselves anymore.

Drugs were our way of rejecting our parents' values, our parents' reality. We really thought, in our naive deception, that we could change the world through our music and our creativity, and we thought that drugs enhanced that creativity. In addition, I personally used drugs to numb the internal pain I carried from the absence of my father in the time of my life when I needed him most. My world became saturated with drugs. For the next ten years, I was literally high all the time.

In 1972, I did session work with Harry Nilsson for his album *Nilsson Schmilsson.* You may remember the odd little Top Ten hit from that album called "Coconut," with its famous lyric "Put the lime in the coconut and drink it all up." I played guitar on that song, and if you'll listen, you'll find that there is only one chord in that entire song, a C7 chord. Despite the simplicity of the song, it took us sixteen hours to record it. Why? Because we were mixing acid and cocaine right there in the studio. We would get started and someone would mess up, and this happened over and over and over. It was funny at first, then it became grueling. Harry ended up lying on the floor trying to sing the song because he was too stoned to stand up.

These days, I jokingly tell people that I am one of the few people in the world who has been to hell and lived to tell about it. Hell, my friends, is playing a C7 chord over and over and over for sixteen hours. To top it all off, the music press of the day hailed the song as a work of genius!

By 1973, Hookfoot had recorded four albums and built a solid fan base among serious connoisseurs of our style of music. Meanwhile,

Elton's popularity had skyrocketed, but it was clear to me that he had deliberately decided to go for a more mainstream pop sound. From *Honky Chateau* to *Don't Shoot Me* to *Goodbye Yellow Brick Road*, I considered the music to be more and more watered down and more and more a compromise of the musical integrity we had worked together to build in his early work. When "Crocodile Rock" came out in 1972, that was it for me. As far as I was concerned, Elton had sold out. I felt that he had moved into a type of music that had nothing to do with me.

The same was true of Gus Dudgeon's production work. Gus was obviously the right producer for Elton—they worked together well and had huge success together. I had great respect for

Gus both as a person and as a producer. Still, we in Hookfoot were never happy with his mixes, because the guitars were mixed down too low and sounded thin. He did this on purpose in order to let Elton's piano take the lead, but in my opinion it was also part of a strategy of homogenizing the music to fit mainstream tastes.

This is another reason I wasn't jealous of Elton's increasing popularity and commercial success. If he wanted to go for a blatantly commercial pop sound, that was his business, and who can argue with the incredible career he has had? But it wasn't to my personal taste.

We never discussed this, because by 1972, Elton and I were on the road and hardly ever saw each other. When we did talk, we were genuinely excited for each other, because we were both living the dream we had worked so hard to achieve. Elton was selling millions of records, selling out concerts, and producing a string of Top Ten hits—it would have been pretty ridiculous for me to tell him that he should be doing things differently. But as for me, I had simply quit listening to his new albums.

    That's not quite as harsh as it sounds, because the fact is that musicians seldom listen to their own albums or the albums they've been involved in. The music business is exciting and glamorous and fun, but it is also a job, and one that involves hard work and long hours. Successful session musicians such as myself end up playing on so many albums that we can't even remember them all. Fans purchase the records and play them over and over and analyze every word and memorize every note, but we don't. To us, it's our job. We show up at the studio, learn the song, play it, then move on to the next track or the next session.

For example, as exciting as the *Elton John* sessions were, the fact is that I only played on four tracks on that album, and I wasn't there when the others were recorded. In that case, we all listened to the finished product because it was such a great album and because we knew it was going to be Elton's jumping-off point, but for most of the albums I've played on, the only time I've heard them is when we were recording them. It's sort of weird, but the fact is that your eyes are always focused on the next project.

This holds true for the artists themselves, not

just the session musicians. It's widely known that Elton tends to write the songs, play his piano part, and then go into another room and watch soccer until it's time to do his vocals. Once he's done this for all the tracks, he leaves, letting the producer and the rest of the band finish their parts, adding backing vocals and layering on other instruments. He comes back in for a final playback, but you can bet he doesn't play his own albums when he's sitting around at home.

Early in his career, Elton said that writing popular songs was like licking a stamp, putting it on an envelope, and sending it off. Davey Johnstone, Elton's lead guitar player, has stated that he doesn't remember how to play any of the songs from the earlier albums unless he practices them to perform in concert. Likewise, Davey tells of the time in 1974 when he had to teach John Lennon the chords to "Lucy in the Sky (With Diamonds)" so he could play on Elton's cover of the song. As shocking as that is, you have to remember that Lennon had written that song in 1966, by which time The Beatles had stopped touring, so Lennon had quite possibly never played the song after it was recorded.

I've been told that fans find all this hard to believe. Think about it this way: If you wrote a novel, you might read over it one time after it came out to make sure there were no typos, but you certainly wouldn't sit down to read it for pleasure. You would go on reading other people's novels, and you would turn your attention to writing your next one.

Likewise, if you're Stephen Speilberg, you don't take the family to see one of your own movies. That would hardly be the way to relax and get your mind off your work. When you did watch movies, you would watch the movies being made by Francis Ford Coppola and George Lucas and the other great directors, because you would want to learn from them and keep up with what was going on in your industry.

So it is with music. Once a song is recorded, it's gone. Unless I played on that particular track, or played it live later, I wouldn't remember it. We listened to music constantly, but what we listened to was either our competition or the earlier music that inspired us, like blues, R&B,

or jazz. It's a dirty little secret of popular music that most of us don't really listen to popular music! We listened to musicians who were of a much higher caliber than we were, because that's who we learned from. Listen to those old Rolling Stones or Led Zeppelin albums and you'll hear the influence of the old blues musicians. You won't hear a shred of influence from Lulu or Sonny & Cher!

People act shocked when I tell them I never even owned an Elton John album after *Madman Across the Water*, but why would I? I didn't play them, and they weren't the kind of music I listened to. Besides, I had access to copies through the record company whenever I wanted them, so why bother keeping them? So, for example, when *Honky Chateau* came out, I heard the album played one time at the record company offices, and that was it. I was so busy with my own band at that time that I didn't give it much thought. To this day I couldn't tell you the tracks on that album.

In 1972, I got married to Patricia, the girl I had been dating for a couple of years. To give you an idea of how crazy my life was, we got married in the middle of a three-month tour of England with Humble Pie. I had to drive 300 miles on a Friday night back to Newcastle from London so we could get married Saturday morning. Elton was there, along with some other pop stars, and that brought the press there in droves. The next day, our wedding was on the front page of the *Daily Express*. I had Sunday off, so that was our honeymoon. On Monday I drove 500 miles to Scotland to go back on the road. This was the beginning of a decade-long period in which I was almost always in a studio or on the road.

Some of you have already noted the irony. I never really knew my father because he was on the road all the time. I didn't like the way he left my mother alone all the time, and I especially hated him for leaving me alone. And how was I starting my marriage? Exactly the same way. Yet I was blind to the hypocrisy. In my mind, I had "made it." Moreover, I was fulfilling my perverse urge to show my father that I could make it "on my own." As in so many other times in my life, Satan blinded me to the fact that I was following the very path that had caused me so much pain when my father had traversed it.

I had met Patricia when she was seventeen, so we had a long friendship/courtship before we got married. At that young age, she was a very insecure person, but she was a good wife during those early years, despite the fact that she must have known that I wasn't being faithful when I was on the road. Of course, we were both doing drugs on a regular basis, because that's just what you did.

Overall, I was pretty satisfied with my career and with my life. But if you look at the lyrics to our songs, you'll see that we were searching. There were songs questioning the existence of God ("Is Anyone There?"), songs attacking organized religion ("Look to Your Churches"), songs about the strain and loneliness of living on the road ("Three Days Out," "Flying in the

U.S.A."), and many songs crying out for peace and love and the hope of future generations ("Communication," "If I Had the Words," "Good Times A'Comin' ").

In retrospect, it's interesting how often God found his way into my lyrics. In "Living in the City," for example, I paint an idyllic picture of a shepherd in the country, looking at the "green hills and rolling fields on a sunny day." The song ends with this line: "The birds call to the source of all that's ever been and gone." In "The Painter," I talk of a young orphan who "never knew religion like the way most people do who went to Sunday school." It's obvious that I wasn't sure whether God was the answer, but my lyrics showed that I was searching for whatever the answer was.

Still, this was the poignant questioning of a young man confident that he would eventually find the answers. In the meantime, I thought I was doing fine.

One day in 1973, I picked up the telephone and heard a voice I hadn't heard in thirteen years. "Hello," the voice said. "It's me. It's your dad. I'm back in town." He still had contacts in the music industry, so he had heard about my success. It was such a shock hearing from him that I didn't have time to feel the anger I harbored toward him, and I agreed to meet him at a pub for a drink. On the train on the way to the pub, all that anger boiled up inside of me, and I prepared myself to tell him off in a major way. "I'm going to kill this guy," I said to myself. But as I was walking down the street toward the pub, I saw him standing on the sidewalk outside, and he was this little shrimp of a guy. He had left when I was twelve, so in my mind's eye he had always seemed big and imposing, but now he was smaller than me and so much older looking. In that instant, all the anger I had for him left me.

Well, not all the anger. The first thing I said after we went inside and sat down was, "Don't expect me to call me you 'Dad.' You haven't earned that right." He accepted this without argument. From then on I called him by his first name, Cab.

Thus began the strangest relationship I've ever had. In hindsight, I see that I still wanted to please my dad, so I became friends with him despite all he had done to me and despite a very unhealthy relationship that developed between us. I began buying drugs from my father in order to have a friendship with him. I thought that the way to get to know him was to get high with him. He would bring his wife over to my house, or I would take my wife over to his house, and we would all get high together. It was just not a healthy time for either of us.

He was going through a terrible time himself, being married to a Nigerian woman who was crazy and who was driving him crazy. She was into witchcraft and such, and they would have terrible fights all the time. She would get drunk or stoned and threaten to jump out of the upstairs window. It was as crazy as my childhood home had ever been, except now the shoe was on the other foot—it was now my father who was trying to protect himself.

Looking back, I see that this was part of the reason I was comfortable being friends with him. I was bigger than he was, I was more successful than he was, and I was living in a nice London flat while he was renting a shabby little place in Nottinghill Gate. Taking him to my house and introducing him to my wife was a way of showing him that I was a man. Smoking pot with him was a way of fulfilling that childhood desire to be like him and his fellow band members. It's all very perverse, but that's the psychology behind it.

He came to a Hookfoot gig, and he enjoyed what we were doing. It was the first time since I won those piano contests as a little boy that he had expressed pride in his son.

The next year, though, Hookfoot broke up. Our eclectic blend of musical styles had doomed us to commercial failure, and the record company had never gotten a handle on how to market us. The members of Hookfoot couldn't have cared less about producing hit singles, and after four albums, I think the record company began to realize this. Investing in break-even or barely profitable albums was fine as long as you're building toward something bigger, but it's hard to justify when the band itself isn't aiming for greater commercial success.

After we broke up, Roger Pope and David Glover joined Kiki Dee's band. I had already made other plans. Earlier that year, I had played on an album for an American artist named Bill Quateman, who was on the CBS label. Quateman's management company was Comtrak, a Chicago firm that also did a thriving business recording jingles for commercials. They had heard my work on Quateman's album, and when they came to England to record some commercial tracks in a studio in Wembley, I was brought in as one of the session musicians. At the end of that session, they asked me if I would be interested in moving to Chicago and working for them. As you can imagine, I had no interest in playing on commercial jingles, but it was a clear ticket to the States and the coveted green card that would allow me to work in the American music industry. I accepted immediately.

The last time I saw my dad before I left, we

were sitting around at his place getting high, and out of the blue I asked, "Cab, do you believe in life after death?"

He shook his head. "No, no. It's just ashes to ashes and dust to dust."

"You really think so?" I asked. I thought for a moment. "You know what?" I said, "I think you're wrong. And one day I'm going to find out."

The next week I moved to Chicago, and I didn't hear from my father for twenty years. When I did, it would be for a reason I never would have guessed.

Chapter Seven

Back With Elton

We arrived in Chicago in March 1974. It took Patricia a long time to get over the culture shock. She hated Chicago, but I assured her we wouldn't be there long. Chicago to me was just a stepping stone to my green card and an eventual music career in Hollywood. As it turned out, we were there less than a year when an unexpected telephone call jump-started our move to L.A.

My job in Chicago with Comtrack was to compose and play on radio and television commercial jingles for everyone from McDonald's to Sears. If you were in America in 1974, you heard my guitar more than once. Obviously, it was the low point as far as my musical integrity was concerned, but, again, I knew all along that it was merely a stepping stone. Also, the company I was working for helped me get session work. I continued to play on Bill Quateman's albums, as well as playing for artists such as Phil Upchurch, Sonny Terry, and Brownie McGee.

What should have been the high point of my time in Chicago came when I was hired to play on an album for legendary bluesman Willie Dixon. For a guitarist with a background in jazz and blues, the idea of playing for such a figure, and doing so right there in Chicago, was as close to the real thing as I would ever get. Willie had his own band, but the producer wanted another guitarist to help fill out the sound. On the scheduled night, I arrived at the address I had been given to find a cheap, eight-track studio in the basement of a drugstore. The producer was just this young kid, and Dixon and his band were nowhere in sight.

After a long wait, a bus pulled up outside, and Willie's band poured in. They had come straight from a show and were still wearing their stage costumes of purple mohair suits. This was the '70s, and I'm surprised there was room for all of us in there with all the Afros. Then Willie walked in wearing his black hat and trench coat. I was amazed at what an enormous man he was. He was about 6' 6", and he had never been a skinny guy. He filled the room all by himself.

Willie pulled out this cheap little portable cassette player and put in a tape. "Gentlemen," he said, "these are the songs. Listen here." He hit the play button, and we all gathered around, trying to hear the music through the distortion of the cheap speakers. When the tape finished, Willie opened his coat wide. In one inside pocket was a bottle of gin; in the other was a revolver. "Gentlemen," he said, "I think we're ready." He took his coat off and sat down, and with that, we started playing.

I was standing next to Willie's lead guitarist, and I started playing along with him. He stopped playing and said, "Hey, I found my part. You go find your own." They obviously didn't want me there, and they weren't going to help me at all.

It turned out that this young producer was convinced he could make Dixon sound more commercial. So here we had one of the greatest living blues legends—a man who had written and produced multiple hit songs for other artists—and this upstart white kid was trying to tell him how to play. He kept stopping the tape in the middle of the songs and saying in this whiny voice, "Uh, Willie, we're trying to make a single here, something that will appeal to the kids, and no one's going to understand that line. Can we change that lyric just a bit?" (If you've ever heard Cheech & Chong's "Blind Melon Chitlin'" sketch from around that time, this was it exactly.) Well, Willie would just lay into him with the worst language you can imagine, just absolutely screaming obscenities at this kid. "Change the #@$*&^% lyrics? I ain't changing no &^*@$#% lyrics for no one!"

This went on until about three o'clock in the

morning. The little studio was thick with marijuana smoke. I found my sound and did my part, but when I left that place, my head was spinning, and not just from the drugs. Ever since I was a little boy, I had longed to enter the exclusive world of the jazz and blues musician. Now I had played with the best, but it had hardly been an inspiring or glamorous experience.

As the cold Chicago winter of 1974 came upon us, Patricia became more and more unhappy about living there, and I felt pretty much the same way. Then one night in January 1975, the telephone rang. It was Elton John, then at the very peak of his success. His first greatest hits album, released just a couple of months before, had become his fifth consecutive number-one album. His next album,

Captain Fantastic and the Brown Dirt Cowboy—an autobiographical album chronicling our early days at Dick James Music on Denmark Street—had just been recorded and was scheduled for release in May. That album would turn out to be the first album ever to ship platinum and the first ever to enter the American pop charts at number one. By various estimates, Elton John records would account for somewhere between two and six percent of worldwide records sales in 1975. He had become, simply stated, the biggest rock star since The Beatles.

Of course, he was still Reg to me. We joked around in our usual way, and I congratulated him on his success. Then he surprised me by telling me that he had fired Dee Murray and Nigel Olsson. I said, "What? Why?" I couldn't believe it. Dee and Nigel had gelled so well with Elton musically in those early days that they seemed inseparable. This was a major shock.

He told me he let them go for two reasons. First, he felt like they were always whining and never quite satisfied with anything. More importantly, he wanted to go in a different direction musically, to rock a little harder and to get back to a looser, less mainstream-pop sound. (Naturally, I was pleased to hear that.) He also wanted to have a bigger band. So, he said, he wanted to bring some of the original guys back together. He told me he'd already contacted Roger Pope, and he wanted to know if I'd be interested in rejoining him. I wanted out of Chicago anyway, and this was my ticket.

Elton was calling from a tennis spa in Scottsdale, Arizona, where he was spending some time relaxing and losing weight by playing tennis with Billie Jean King. He offered to fly me out to discuss the details. I arrived and was reunited with Elton, his manager John Reid, his guitarist Davey Johnstone, and others. It was very relaxed and quiet there, and our discussion was very casual.

Elton assured me that he wanted to take a looser, funkier approach with his music. I let him know what he already knew—that I despised some of the mainstream pop songs he had recently produced. In fact, I set one condition on my returning to his band: I would not play "Crocodile Rock." That's why, for the next two tours, Elton didn't play one of his biggest hits. I sat down with

John Reid, Elton's manager, to work out the business details. I don't remember the exact amount of money I was offered, but let's just say it was a paradigm shift in my lifestyle at that time. I didn't hesitate to sign the contract.

Patricia and I packed our stuff, paid off our apartment lease, and joined the rest of the band in Amsterdam to rehearse for the *Captain Fantastic* tour. We were there for a whole month, staying at the Amsterdam Hilton. The practice sessions were excellent; the new band gelled right away. We were playing some hot stuff. I don't remember any struggles musically or otherwise during this time. We were all excited to be involved in the project and to be part of the band.

It was a great rehearsal, but it was also

major party time. Other rock stars like Keith Moon and Ringo Starr would drop by. It got pretty wild. We had our wives and girlfriends with us, so there were no groupies hanging around, but it was during this time that my drug use went up to the next level. At one point, I went on a four-day cocaine binge with Ringo, and during that time I asked him a question about the *Sgt. Pepper's Lonely Hearts Club Band* album. Ringo was so stoned that he couldn't remember the album.

It was also during this time that Ringo asked if he could join Elton's band. "I'm not doing anything right now," he said in front of the whole group. "How about letting me go on tour with you?" He was serious, but he was also high as a kite at the time. We all just looked at each other with embarrassment. We already had a drummer for the band, but how do you politely turn down a Beatle? I think it was John Reid who finally pulled him aside and explained things to him.

    The new band consisted of Davey Johnstone and me on guitar, Roger Pope on drums, Ray Cooper on percussion, and two new guys—James Newton Howard on keyboards and Kenny Passerelli on bass. James had produced Ringo's 1974 *Goodnight Vienna*, to which Elton and Bernie had contributed the song "Snookeroo" and on which Elton had performed. Kenny Passerelli had played with Stephen Stills and Joe Walsh and had co-written Walsh's 1973 megahit, "Rocky Mountain Way." It was James and Kenny who brought the cocaine thing into the band in a major way, but that's not to suggest that the rest of us were innocent in that regard.

The first gig of the British tour was at Wembley Stadium on June 21, 1975. We were the last act of a day-long festival that included The Beach Boys, the Eagles, and others. Elton had decided that we would play the entire *Captain Fantastic* album through in order as our way of introducing it to the world. One music critic wrote that the audience was bored and began walking out on us, but if that's true, we certainly didn't notice it from the stage. It looked to us like we were getting a positive and attentive response.

Patricia and I had given up the apartment in Chicago, so she went with me in July to the Caribou recording studio in Colorado to record the new album. We all stayed in the cabins there at the ranch, living and working together for several weeks. Kenny Passerelli had a house in Boulder, so he stayed there. One day when Patricia and I went to visit him, we found Maxine Taupin—Bernie's wife and the one who had inspired the song "Tiny Dancer"—living there with him. She had just moved out from Bernie and in with Kenny. Of course, Bernie was there in the studios along with Kenny, but if there was any tension, I don't remember it. I do know that Bernie was drinking pretty heavily during that period, and that he was keeping to himself even more than usual, but you have to understand how we looked at things back then. This was not a Christian frame of reference. It was the '70s; it was a group that was heavily into drugs and free love; there were so many women in and out of our lives. So Maxine had left Bernie and moved in with Kenny—so what? We didn't give it a second thought. "If it feels good, do it."

Rejoining Elton gave Patricia and me the money we needed to move out to Los Angeles, so before the American leg of the tour started in the fall, we went out to L.A. and found an apartment. Patricia was thrilled. She had hated Chicago, but she loved it in L.A. She wasn't working, and over the coming months she really began to enjoy the trappings of success. She became more outgoing and less passive, something I saw as a positive change, until it came back to slap me in the face.

All the dates for the fall tour were on the West Coast, and on the album we had just recorded, we had purposefully emulated the West Coast rock sounds of groups like The Eagles. Elton, always ready with a pun, turned the phrase "west of the Rockies" into *Rock of the Westies*, and that became the name of the album and the tour. The tour culminated with the two sold-out shows at Dodger Stadium, the first band to appear there since The Beatles.

For the next year, we conducted the most successful rock & roll tour that had ever taken place up to that point. Everywhere we went, we sold out, and everywhere we went, the top celebrities of the day found their way backstage. I remember standing backstage at Madison Square Garden and looking over and seeing Leonard Nimoy—Mr. Spock of *Star Trek*—talking with Liza Manelli. I was twenty-five years old, making more money than I knew what to do with, and hanging around with celebrities like Billie Jean King, Ringo Starr, and actor Richard Thomas, who at that time was playing "John-Boy" on *The Waltons*.

So it got a bit surrealistic at times, but we had great fun. It was a time of tremendous excitement; I can't deny that. I enjoyed working with Davey Johnstone, Roger Pope, Kenny Passerelli, and the other members of the band. We built strong relationships during that time.

Unlike the other members of that band, my picture had appeared on the covers of both the *Elton John* and *Tumbleweed Connection* albums, and I had been listed in the credits of both *Friends* and *Madman Across the Water*. Of those in the new lineup, only Davey Johnstone had been pictured or listed on more Elton John albums. I was also pictured along with the rest of the band on the cover of the new album, all of which made me almost as much of a celebrity among Elton John fans as Elton himself. During the tour, I was recognized on the street and in the hotel, and girls in the audience would scream for me by name. The interest in Elton and the desire to see him was nothing less than frenzied, and for the first time I found myself becoming a prisoner of the hotel room.

We'd made it. We'd achieved the dreams we'd started dreaming as kids back in the mid-'60s. This was the peak. This was as good as it was ever going to get for a rock & roll act.

Playing with the hottest artist in pop music,

our choices were unlimited when it came to women. When my wife wasn't with me, the groupies were. With Elton it was straight off the stage, into the limo, and back to the hotel. We'd all go to the hospitality suite to wind down from the show, and the roadies would bring a whole passel of women into the party. Sometimes the women would get to the hotel on their own and even find out which floor we were on. Women would sometimes come in specifically looking for a certain band member, but most weren't so picky. After a little talking and drinking, we'd pair off and go to our rooms to get high and have sex. It was like that night after night, in city after city.

    At that time, it wasn't public knowledge that Elton was gay, so women were always showing up hoping to go to bed with him. But Elton would only show his face in the hospitality suite for a few minutes, then disappear. He had his own crowd with him then, and they would basically have their own party in a different room.

As I said, it was during this time that the drugs really got bad. We were making such vast amounts of money that we could afford to buy as much as we could put into our bodies. What had once been a bad habit became a way of life. Throughout the mid- to late-'70s, I was literally high all the time. Only another former drug addict will understand what I mean when I say that I would get so high that I was straight.

With Hookfoot, we had gotten our drugs through local dealers that someone in the band knew, but with Elton we entered a whole new world. There were two major drug dealers from Miami who would meet us at every hotel. These were high-level guys, the kind who had boats and planes and mansions in Miami. They were two athletic-looking guys about our age, always wearing sporty casual clothes and always tanned. As soon as we got into our hotel rooms in each new city, we'd receive a phone call from these guys telling us which room they were in. We'd go down there and they would open up suitcases full of cocaine and other drugs. Each of us would lay down thousands of dollars in cash for whatever we needed to tide us over until the next time.

    The easy money and the easy drug access combined to help me develop a cocaine habit that was costing me a small fortune every week. In addition, we were almost always given a little vial of cocaine just before we went on stage. "Here you go, boys. Do a good show!"

In every drinking crowd, there's always one guy who can drink everyone else under the table. In Elton's group, I was the guy that could do more coke, smoke more pot, pop more pills, and drop more acid than anyone else and still play my guitar. Drugs had been part and parcel of the music business at least since my grandfather's day, and the higher up you go, the more there is. At the level where we were, the supply was virtually unlimited, a very dangerous situation.

I used to snort cocaine off the top of my amplifier on stage in the middle of songs. At that time it was the hip thing to have dry ice "smoke" come out over the stage during a song like "Funeral For a Friend." We loved this, because it allowed us to get high on stage without anyone seeing us. The lights would dim and the roadies would pump the mist in from the side of the stage, and while the audience was mesmerized, I would walk back and just fill my face up off the top of my amp. Then I'd come back and play more raving guitar riffs and the crowd would just go wild. Back then, it seemed like the perfect setup.

But things were not perfect in my life. On the surface, it looked like things couldn't be better. People I had known for a long time would say, "Oh, Caleb, that's great. You've really made it now." We were doing four-hour shows with one twenty-minute intermission, and they were very, very tiring shows. I would go back to my hotel room still in my stage clothes and still sweating. In my ears would be the echo of the applause. Waiting in the hospitality suite would be the adoring groupies. But deep down in my soul, there was a huge hole that could not be filled by all the success, all the adulation, all the money, all the drugs, all the women. I would just stand and look at myself in the mirror, and I would say, "Is this it? Is this making it? There's got to be more to it than this."

I wasn't the only one having difficulties in the midst of all the hoopla. It was during the 1975 tour that Elton tried to commit suicide by swallowing all those pills just before the Dodger Stadium shows. And Maxine Taupin had apparently decided to stay with Kenny Passerelli for the time being, so she and Bernie had filed for divorce. As a result, when we went to Toronto to record the next album, Bernie didn't come with us, and the lyrics he gave Elton were so depressing that the album ended up being called *Blue Moves*.

Blue Moves would be Elton's first album out from under Dick James Music, so he wanted to get it right. He wanted the band to work together to develop the songs, and several of them are the result of impromptu hotel room jams. That's why there are multiple composing credits on some of the tracks. Elton and Gus Dudgeon brought in The Beach Boys, The Captain and Tenille, David Sanborn, David Crosby, and my old friend Graham Nash. Gus even went out to L.A. to record backing vocals by the Reverend James Cleveland's Cornerstone Institutional Baptist and Southern Californian Community Choir, which had performed with us at Dodger Stadium. The goal was to create another double album that would repeat the success of *Goodbye Yellow Brick Road*.

It was all to no avail. When it was finished, we all agreed that there was barely enough good material there for a single album, and Gus was directed to edit the material appropriately.

The main problem was that the lyrics were almost all depressing, and no one wants to listen to a double album full of slow, sad songs. In addition, Elton was clearly beginning to suffer from burnout (and who could blame him?), so his melodies didn't have their usual sparkle. But the biggest problem, in my opinion, was that Gus Dudgeon had once again mixed the guitars down too low. The basic tracks of the album would have kicked the walls down, but the final version sounded thin. The same had been true with *Rock of the Westies*. The band kicked a whole lot harder when it played live than what you hear on the records.

Although Elton now had a contract with MCA Records, he had also started his own record company for the purpose of launching other acts. The first performer to be signed to Rocket Records was Kiki Dee, and Elton was going to ensure her success by recording a duet with her during the *Blue Moves* sessions. Kiki had been a backup singer in England in those early days on Denmark Street, but I had never met her. In 1974, however, she had had a number-twelve hit with "I've Got the Music in Me" (with Roger Pope playing drums), so we all looked forward to working with her.

As it turns out, I still didn't meet her, because she didn't attend the *Blue Moves* sessions. Instead, Elton and Bernie wrote this song called "Don't Go Breaking My Heart" and we recorded the music. Elton then recorded his portion of the vocal, and Gus Dudgeon took the tapes back to England to record Kiki's portion. I finally met her when she started dating Davey Johnstone and went out on the road with us occasionally.

"Don't Go Breaking My Heart"—released as a one-off single and not included on the album—was a monster smash hit worldwide. In fact, it became Elton's first ever number-one hit in

England. And while the song made Kiki Dee's name a household word, I'm not sure that it didn't ultimately hurt her career. Songs like "I've Got the Music in Me" were true rock songs that she sang with real soul, which is why she was the first white artist from the UK signed by Motown. The massive success of "Don't Go Breaking My Heart" froze her in the public's mind as a light disco pop singer, similar to an actor getting typecast in a certain role in a television show.

    Kiki is an excellent singer and a very nice lady—a down-to-earth Yorkshire girl. In fact, she may have been a little too down-to-earth for a career in rock & roll, especially in those glam rock days. Whatever it was, it's my opinion that her career never reached the heights her talent deserves.

With the album in the can, we went to England for what Elton dubbed the "Louder than Concorde, But Not Quite as Pretty" tour. We played a different city almost every night throughout the month of May. In August, it was back to America for a record-setting seven straight sold-out concerts in Madison Square Garden.

But as with the year before, there was trouble in paradise. Elton was burned out. It was no surprise. He had been working almost nonstop for the past ten years. Since 1970, he had produced two studio albums a year, two of them double albums, for a total of thirteen albums! He had been touring almost constantly, in addition to the publicity demands of being one of the world's top stars. Like me, he had been taking an increasing amount of drugs as part of this daily routine. It was only a matter of time before the strain began to show.

In retrospect, it began to show on the first day of the *Blue Moves* sessions. We started with a rocker called "Bite Your Lip (Get Up and Dance)." We ran through it one time just to get the sound down, then Elton stood up and said, "That's a wrap. That'll be a hit." Gus Dudgeon told him we didn't have a final take on the song yet, but Elton refused to do it over, insisting that it was fine the way it is. A seasoned professional like Elton knew better. This was the first take of the sessions; no matter how good the band may have sounded, there was no way that Gus could have had everything in the control room set the way it needed to be. Elton's refusal to do the song over was unusual behavior for a performer known to be the consummate perfectionist.

Then, while we were in New York playing Madison Square Garden, Elton was interviewed by Cliff Jahr of *Rolling Stone* magazine. There had been mild rumors about Elton's sexual orientation for years, but no one had ever published these rumors, nor had anyone asked him about them directly. In the course of this interview, the subject came up, and Elton readily admitted that he was "bisexual." The interview was scheduled to be published as the cover story of the October issue.

In 1976, as far as I know, no major star had ever publicly admitted being bisexual. It will seem strange to young people today, when gay rights are talked about all the time, but back then it was *verboten*. I'm sure that Elton's admission sent shivers down the spine of his manager, John Reid. Reid was gay himself, but as a manager and public relations expert, he knew the damage this interview could cause.

Perhaps Elton's casual admission of his sexual orientation was a sign of the strain he had been under; perhaps it was just Elton being his usual frank self. All I know is that, one day during the Madison Square Garden run, Reid told us that Elton was going to retire temporarily. There would be no more touring for a while, and he wasn't even sure when he was going to do the next album. We were all shocked. Roger Pope was especially upset, because he had flown his parents over from England for the first time to witness his success, and here the carpet had been yanked right out from under him. He proceeded to go back to the Waldorf Astoria and trash his room in true rock star fashion.

Meanwhile, Gus Dudgeon had made a mistake. At a luncheon to introduce him to the MCA executives, he let it slip that we had recorded enough songs for a double album, but that he was going to edit it down to a single disc. Almost immediately the word came down that MCA wanted that double album, and Gus was left with no choice but to include material that would normally have been omitted as substandard. When *Blue Moves* was released in October 1976, coinciding with the release of the *Rolling Stone* interview, it stopped cold Elton's string of number-one albums.

Don't get me wrong; the album isn't a complete disaster. It has some good music on it, including three instrumental tracks. The first single, "Sorry Seems to be the Hardest Word," climbed to number six in America and number eleven in England, and different second singles entered the Top Thirty in each country. The album went gold in its first month and platinum by the end of the year, but that was mainly because people at that time just went out and bought whatever Elton put out. This time people were disappointed, and as the word got out, the album peaked at number three in both America and England, then slid quickly down the charts. It would be two years before Elton would release another studio album.

So my gig with Elton was over, at least for

the time being. I went home to Los Angeles and began looking for session work. I hooked up with Davlen Studios in Studio City (which is no longer going), and they assigned me work whenever I was in town. The first project I worked on was a solo album by Bruce Johnstone of The Beach Boys. (Bruce had sung on several of Elton's songs, including "Don't Let the Sun Go Down on Me." He had also sung on *Blue Moves*, which was when I got to know him.) Over the next couple of years, I did session work with jazz trumpet player Eddie Henderson, jazz keyboardist Patrice Russian, Alphonso Johnson (former bass player for Weather Report and Santana), Dusty Springfield, John Klemmer, and others.

On February 6, 1977, Patricia and I had a

daughter named Lucille. When Lucille was born, I was in the studio doing an album for Liza Minnelli. I got a call from the hospital telling me to get there quick because my daughter was being born. I don't think I was a bad father overall, but that was only because I had the money to hide the negative effects of my drug habit. Believe it or not, I remember holding my infant daughter in one arm while I bent over the dining room table and snorted lines of cocaine off a mirror. Obviously, I wasn't living life through the lens of a husband and father, but of stardom and rock & roll.

My mother and I had remained close until I moved to America, after which our contact had necessarily been limited to long distance telephone calls. That year, I flew her over to see her new granddaughter. I was taking drugs openly while she was there. Remember, my father and his bandmates had smoked marijuana openly in our home when I was growing up, and I had regularly gotten high with my father after he had come back into my life in 1973. I didn't think a thing about snorting cocaine in front of my mother, and as mothers often do, she never condemned my behavior. Needless to say, today I look back on my behavior at that time with shame, and see it as a sign of just how lost I was.

Later in 1977, Roger Pope, Kenny Passarelli, and I were asked to join Hall & Oates. Daryl Hall and John Oates had just had three consecutive Top Ten hits—"Sara Smile," "Rich Girl," and "She's Gone"—all in one year, so they were one of the hottest acts going. Nevertheless, I wasn't excited about playing for them because their music, in my opinion, was a watered-down, pseudo-Philadelphia soul that was so tightly structured that there was no room for any improvisation. Unfortunately, by that time I had developed a lifestyle to which I had become accustomed, including a house in Studio City with a swimming pool and my own recording studio, and a cocaine habit that cost me hundreds of dollars a day. So I took the gig.

The atmosphere with Hall & Oates was not very pleasant. I felt that we were treated like animals rather than people, sent out on the road for six months without a break to promote the latest record. It seemed like there were always shady-looking characters from New York flying in and hanging around, and I noticed that some of them carried guns. I never did understand their connection to the band. I guess they were "investors," coming out on the road to check on the "product," which was us.

And now we were being supplied with all the drugs we needed without charge. "You okay, boys? Anything you need?" When you're paying for your own drugs, you at least have an idea of how big your habit is, because you know how much you've spent. When they're being supplied for free, there's no way—and no reason—to keep track. From that point on, I couldn't even begin to tell you how much cocaine I was snorting.

Once, after a Hall & Oates concert, I was

standing backstage with the rest of the band and the usual group of hangers-on, when a woman walked up to me with two young girls at her side. She introduced the girls to me as her daughters, then told me that all three of them would spend the night with me if I wanted. Now, I was no Puritan, but something inside me was repelled by the sickness of this suggestion. I'm not even sure the girls were of legal age. I just laughed nervously and passed them off to one of the roadies to be escorted out.

Events like this were starting to make me realize that I was becoming dissatisfied with the rock & roll lifestyle. The euphoria had begun to wear off. The dream was still alive, but it was getting frayed around the edges, because reality wasn't living up to the dream. I had played with the best of the best, I had played in the biggest stadiums, I had taken every kind of drug and had every kind of woman, and still I found myself standing in front of the mirror saying, "There's got to be more to it than this."

As the music industry had grown, and as I had risen in it, it had become more and more about business and less and less about artistic expression. I couldn't make any money playing the music I really believed in, and I couldn't be proud of myself playing the kind of music that made money. All those obscene amounts of money I had made off of rock & roll had been wasted on the drugs that were so much a part of the rock & roll lifestyle. The gilded cage was closing in on me, and it looked less gilded every day. Now, when I looked in the mirror,

I added a line to my usual statement. I found myself saying, "This isn't fun anymore."

That's when God spoke to me.

Chapter Eight

Hotel Damascus

It happened on October 9, 1979, my thirtieth birthday. I had been on the road with Hall & Oates for six months straight. We played the Omni Theatre in Atlanta, Georgia, and after the concert, the band threw a surprise birthday party for me back in my hotel room. The roadies brought in cake, booze, women, and cocaine, and we just all went nuts until around five in the morning. When it finally ended, I was left alone in my hotel room. I sat there alone in a chair, just cooling off before getting into bed. I wasn't thinking about anything in particular, when all of a sudden I heard a voice. It was a voice I had never heard before, and it was so loud and so clear that it seemed to come from inside of me and from outside of me at the same time.

"*Caleb,*" the voice said, "*from this point on, your life is going to be completely different. Nothing is going to be the same for you ever again.*"

I snapped up straight and said out loud, "Who's that?" The voice was so clear that I actually turned around to see who was standing behind me. The only thing behind me was the hotel window—we were on the ninth floor of the Omni Hotel.

I had no idea who the voice belonged to, but I knew something significant had happened. I made a promise to myself to find out more, but I didn't know where to begin. I had grown up in the church and I had attended Anglican Church schools, but with all the fancy sermons I had heard condemning every kind of sin, I had never heard the gospel preached. I was never told that I could have a personal relationship with God or with Jesus. I knew God was out there somewhere—I was never an atheist—but I didn't know what it meant to have a relationship with God.

That week, whenever someone asked me what I did on my birthday, I would innocently tell them about hearing a voice telling me that things were about to change. And they'd say to me, "Oh, that was just the drugs. That voice was just a hallucination." Well, all I can tell you is what I heard, and this voice cut *through* the drugs. Remember, I had years of experience with heavy drug use. I knew a hallucination when I had one. I knew that I had been spoken to that night.

Now, I didn't expect my friends to take my story as proof that God exists, but it did seem odd to me that they so readily assumed that He could not have spoken to me that night. I guess they thought they were being all rational and scientific, but I would suggest that they were being *ir*rational and *un*scientific. If the existence of God cannot be scientifically proven, neither can it be scientifically disproven. It is one thing to say, "Oh, I know Caleb, and he was a drug addict and came from a messed-up family, and I just don't believe what he says." It's another thing to say that God could not have spoken to me that night. The assumption that God doesn't exist is at least as unscientific as the belief that He does, and even more so when it leads people to ignore clear evidence in His creation that points to His handiwork.

Belief in God is a matter of faith, but when God manifests himself in your life as He did in mine, then that faith is based on evidence. While I may be the only person who heard the evidence in my own life, I am one of millions— throughout centuries, across cultural and political boundaries, and around the world—who have heard the voice of God. Millions alive today claim to feel the presence of the Lord in their lives. How arrogant—and how unscientific—to say that all these people are hallucinating just because you yourself have not felt that presence. Personally, if millions of other people felt something that I wasn't feeling, I'd be curious about it, and try to find out how I might feel it myself. But such is not the case with our skeptical generation.

Of course, it's not just our generation. It goes back to the time of Jesus himself. Not all the disciples believed at first, even when they saw Him perform miracles. Many, many people saw Jesus perform miracles, and many, many more heard first-hand accounts from people they could trust, and yet they turned away. If people standing before the Presence himself did not believe, it's no wonder that many today do not. The question of faith is the same today as it was for those who saw Jesus in person.

Yes, the voice I heard might have been a hallucination, but why would a hallucination tell me that my life was about to change? Other people said it was just my subconscious speaking to me, but why would I address myself in the third person? Others have said that my life had just gotten so bad that I was crying out to God as a last resort. But my life *hadn't* gotten that bad—as far as I was concerned, I was still on the top of the world when this happened. It's true that I was becoming disillusioned with the rock & roll lifestyle, but I was still living the dream I had wanted for so long. It's only in looking back at it now that I realize how empty I felt. Besides, I didn't cry out to God at all. I just heard a voice tell me that my life was about to change.

    Whatever other people want to believe, I know that I wasn't alone in that room that night. Most importantly, my experience was confirmed by the fact that what the voice said turned out to be prophetic. Things really did change in my life and, as you will see, they did not change through any effort of my own, but through circumstances totally beyond my control.

At the end of that tour in 1979, the band members went their separate ways. It was around Christmas, and I went home. In Los Angeles, I had been living the rock & roll dream. I had a house in Laurel Canyon with my own recording studio in it. I had a swimming pool and fancy cars and lots of money. I had a beautiful wife and a lovely daughter. But from the moment I got home at the end of 1979, everything in my life—and I do mean everything—fell apart.

One day several months before, my wife Patricia had made a strange comment to me. "I want my independence," she had said. I remember thinking, "What does that mean? She's got everything she could want, and she's free to do whatever she wants." Back out on the road several weeks later, I was in New York when I ran into a percussionist friend of mine named Lenny Castro. Lenny said, "Man, you better get back home. Your wife is seeing someone else."

Given all the flings I had had on the road, I hardly had any right to judge her, and I was admittedly absorbed in my career and always away from home. But I was shocked to learn that the man with whom she was involved was none other than Bill Quateman, the man whose records had brought us to America. After Patricia and I left Chicago, Quateman had also moved to L.A., and I had continued to play on his projects. He was supposedly one of my best friends. Little did I know that he and my wife had been having an affair.

As they say, there are two sides to every riverbank. On the one hand, I felt hurt and betrayed. On the other hand, had I been a better husband, it might never have happened. Anyway, we were divorced, and they later got married.

My wife leaving me was just the beginning. People stole money from me. The calls for studio work dried up. Despite having all the trappings of wealth, I was cash poor, with nothing invested and nothing in savings. In 1980, I had to declare bankruptcy. In 1982, I had to sell my house.

All this made me grow more and more

dependent on drugs. Six years after playing those Dodger Stadium concerts with Elton, and two years after being on the road with Hall & Oates at the peak of their success, I was sharing a rental house with another guy, and we were dealing drugs out of it for a living.

This was the lowest point of my life. For a year and a half, people would be knocking on our door at all hours of the day and night to get their drugs. How we escaped getting arrested, I'll never know. The worst part of it was, these poor stoned junkies always wanted you to be their therapist. I guess it didn't dawn on them that all the problems they were whining about might go away if they stopped taking drugs and sitting up until daybreak talking with their dealer about the mysteries of the universe.

Of course, in my mind, the drug dealing was just a temporary thing. I just assumed that I would soon be back on top in the rock world. In the late '70s, Roger Pope and I tried to start a new band named The Troops, but it went nowhere. We recorded some great demos and impressed audiences when we played the L.A. clubs, but I made the mistake of letting my stepbrother act as our manager. We found out later that he had been going around making outrageous demands and generally ticking people off, which explains why we never got a recording contract.

In 1981, I was invited by my friend Alphonso Johnson, former bassist for Weather Report, to join a band he was starting with Chester

Thompson, a former drummer for Genesis and, earlier, for Weather Report. We put together a kind of funk/fusion band, and we used to play concerts down by the beach at Pasquale's in Malibu and places like that.

Chester, I came to find out, was a Christian. Now, I knew Christianity only as a ceremonial thing from my childhood, and by that time I had numbed my soul with drugs so much that I wasn't even searching for anything anymore. But there was something about Chester's life that was catching my attention. Here we were, two guys the same age, both of us in the music business for years, and he wasn't crazy. There was a peace and a solidity about his life that I had never had. And I couldn't help but think, "Whatever this guy's got, I want it."

Chester was smart. He never really witnessed to me in an overt fashion, but when the conversation turned to life's bigger questions, Chester would simply and honestly state what God had done in his life. I'm afraid I wasn't as open as Chester, because I was still responding with all the humanistic arguments I had learned as a teenager. You know the ones: "If God made potatoes and cabbages, then he made marijuana, too, so it's okay to smoke marijuana. Like, it all comes from the same earth, man, so it's all groovy." Chester would just smile patiently. We both knew that no matter how good my arguments sounded, I wasn't a happy person.

In fact, my life was spiraling down into the abyss. I was dealing drugs; I was trying to sell guitars; I was miserable; I was lonely; I was going crazy. What might have happened to me, I don't know, but I do know that all the ingredients were there for tragedy.

Then, one day in 1982, Chester called me and asked, "What are you doing today?" I had been up all night with people banging on the door for their drugs, and I was wired.

I said, "Not much, why?"

"Why don't you come to church today?" he asked. "It's Easter."

Well, I didn't even know that it was Sunday, much less that it was Easter. But as soon as he asked me to church, my brain turned 180 degrees, and I thought, "I've tried everything else. Why not church?" So Chester came and picked me up and took me to The Church on the Way in Van Nuys, California.

You should have seen me as I walked into this place. I hadn't been in a church in twenty years, and the last church I had been in had been my local church in Finchley, England, a tiny Anglican church built in the 12th century. If you had twenty people in that church, you had a revival. As an Englishman, I was used to creeping in and picking up a prayer card and whispering a prayer from the card. I was used to a very holy and a very quiet atmosphere in church.

Imagine my reaction when I walked into The Church on the Way with Chester and his wife and saw 2,000 people standing with their hands raised, singing and shouting out praises to God. Up front a huge orchestra was set up for the Easter special. I heard the choir singing over this tremendous sound system—we walked by the soundboard toward the back of the sanctuary and it looked like the soundboards we had used in concerts. I remember wondering if these sound engineers got paid union scale to worship God. And all I could keep thinking as I looked around was, "This is a church?"

So we found our seats and I just kept looking around to see what was going on. I remember that they started singing a chorus, and I still remember today that it was "In My Life Lord, Be Glorified." I had never heard that song before, but somehow it cut into my heart. Something about the sound of their voices and the passion with which they were singing touched me deeply. And as I was sitting there, I heard that voice again, the one from the hotel room. It said, *"Caleb, it's time for you to come home to me today. I've got a new life for you."* And that's when I realized who the voice belonged to. It belonged to Jesus Christ.

All of a sudden I couldn't move in my seat, because the peace of God had fallen all over me. It was like someone had poured a bucket of warm honey over me. I suddenly found a place where I could finally rest my soul. I found a resting place for my pain, for my hurt. I suddenly came to this place where my searching was over. For the first time in my life, I had found a home where I was really loved and a Father who cared. I didn't know what to make of it. I sat there and I physically couldn't move.

And I saw right then how I had been living a lie. Music and drugs had been my gods. Because of the public life I had led—being on stage and on television, meeting famous people, having women throw themselves at me—I had been living on pride. I had been living on pride because of what I could do with a guitar. Everything I had achieved I had credited to myself. I had faith only in myself. But now I saw what a lie that had been. I saw clearly what a mess I had made of things by trying to do them on my own.

On my own. My father's words came back ringing in my ears: "You're on your own now." But now Jesus was speaking to me and telling me that I wasn't on my own anymore. He was telling me that

I had a home, that I had love. I didn't realize how my soul had been aching to hear those words until I heard them. I just sat there and I was struck dumb.

The pastor, Jack Hayford, got up and began to preach a sermon. I don't know to this day what his topic was, but it seemed as though he was telling my whole life's story to the congregation. Everything he said seemed to apply directly to me. I was sitting there thinking, "This man has read my book and I don't even know him!"

At the end of his sermon, he gave an invitation. He had everyone bow their heads and close their eyes. Then he said, "If anyone would like to receive Jesus Christ, would you just lift up your eyes to meet mine and raise your hand?" Well, I stood up and I didn't even know I was standing up. I was standing up and waving my hand above my head. My friend Chester and his wife had their heads bowed, but they felt me moving beside them and glanced up, and when they realized what was happening, they began to weep. I was led forward into a prayer room where a pastor prayed for me and then gave me some literature telling me how to be a Christian.

I gave my life to Jesus that day, but that didn't mean the struggle was over. Because after that I had to go home, and home was the pit of hell. Home was the den of drug dealing. I had to go home and keep living my life, and there was no one there to support me or care about me. So I went home and I ended up carrying on just the way I had before. I was back with people banging on the door at four o'clock in the morning. So I slid away. I slid away from church for a while. I didn't realize it at the time, but I was about to learn a valuable lesson. I was about to learn that there is a difference between accepting Jesus Christ as our Savior and accepting Him as Lord.

    The wake-up call came about three weeks later. Suddenly I became ill. I had always been a strong guy and very healthy, and I never used to get ill, but now I became so ill I couldn't move. I lay on my bed for three days and I almost died. I was so sick I was shaking violently on that bed for three days. I thought my heart was going to pound out of my chest. No one came to see me. No one called. It was an ordeal to get off the bed to go to the bathroom. Seventeen years of doing drugs had taken their toll, and my nervous system was fried. For the first time, I realized my mortality. I realized how weak I was, how weak we all are. As I lay there in agony, I seriously thought, "This is it."

For three days I laid there, and while I did, God showed me a vision of my whole life. It was like a movie running across the ceiling. God showed me my whole life from my earliest childhood up to that present day. He showed me everything I had ever done. He showed me my dreams and my accomplishments, but He also showed me my sins and my failures. And when I saw it all together—when I looked at the big picture —I realized that the accomplishments meant nothing. The fame and fortune had been so fleeting, like smoke in my hands. All my accomplishments had already turned to dust, and after they had passed, they had left me worse off than I had been before. They had left me with a drug addiction; they had left me with a broken marriage; they had left me bankrupt.

Rock & roll could not save me. My friends and family could not save me. Most importantly, I could not save myself. I couldn't even run my own life without messing everything up and squandering everything I had. I couldn't do it on my own.

Twenty years earlier, I had vowed to prove —to my father and to myself—that I could make it on my own. But now, as I lay there in my bed watching this vision of my life gliding across my eyes, I saw that I could not make it on my own. I saw that I had been wrong.

In fact, I saw that my whole generation had been wrong. We had all placed an emphasis on being independent—of handling life "on our own." We had all believed that each person is able to decide what is right or wrong for him or herself. My generation didn't need the church, or our parents, or the government, or our college administrators, or the police telling us what to do. We could make our own decisions.

Well, now that my generation has had its way for fifty years, I can't name one way we have left society better off than it was before. Have we stopped crime, or poverty, or war? Have we cured racism or stopped the sexual exploitation of women? No, almost every social problem of the past is worse than it used to be, and my generation has surely contributed to the worsening situation by insisting that everyone could make the right decisions on their own.

I remember when the sexual revolution started in the 1960s. The mantra of that movement was that "mature, consenting adults" could make responsible decisions on their own. Court decisions such as the legalization of abortion were based on the idea that people were smart enough to make the right decisions for themselves. But if that's true, why are so many abortions—about 1.4 million—performed every year in a country in which birth control is inexpensive and widely available? Does that sound like a lot of mature people making intelligent choices?

No, the fact is that people will often make

the wrong decisions when left on their own. God was showing me how true this had been in my own life. Like everyone else, I liked to think that I was in control, but I wasn't. What God showed me as I lay there completely changed my view of myself and my relationship to the world and to God.

The only way I can explain it is to use an example from the Bible, but I want to stress that you don't have to be a Christian to understand what I'm about to say. Many people who do not believe in the theology presented by the Bible still agree that it is a book of great wisdom. The example I'm about to give is one in which the wisdom shines through even if you don't accept the theology.

As you probably know, the story of Adam and Eve is at the beginning of the Bible. Adam and

Eve were created in God's image, meaning that they were created pure and sinless. Because they were pure and sinless, they could speak directly with God. God would even come down and walk with them in the Garden of Eden. If they wanted to know what to do, all they had to do was ask God.

Then they committed the first sin—they ate the fruit that God had forbidden them to eat. When their sinful natures emerged, they became ashamed of their nakedness. They "fell from grace," and their sin separated them from God. Ever since, man has been the victim of his own sinful nature, and his separation from God keeps him from clearly discerning God's will. This makes him incapable of making the right decisions consistently.

But here's the eerie part. Do you know what

the apple was that Adam and Eve ate? It wasn't just any old fruit. It was fruit from the "Tree of the Knowledge of Good and Evil." And when the serpent was tempting Eve to eat the apple, do you know what he said? He said, "If you eat of the fruit of this tree, you will be like God, knowing good from evil." In other words, you won't need God to tell you what to do, because you will know *on your own*. You will be in control, able to decide for yourself. Exactly what people are still telling themselves today! Of course, it was a false promise then, and it's a false promise today.

Now, let's say you don't believe there ever was an Adam and Eve or a Garden of Eden. Let's say you're one of those people who believe that the stories in the Bible are just myths, stories designed to teach us lessons. I would point out to you that the lesson remains the same: men and women have sinful natures that render them incapable of making proper decisions on a consistent basis.

People today don't like to believe that we have a dark side to our natures. We like to believe that people are "basically good," and Christianity is always being criticized for focusing on the negative. But it is not just Christianity that teaches that we are a mixture of good and evil. Buddhists talk of the "yin and yang," and their symbol for that concept shows the dark and light swirling around and invading each other. Plato spoke of our conflicting natures. George Lucas built his classic *Star Wars* movie series around the idea of a universal "Force" that has a "Dark Side" as well as a good side, and the success of those movies suggests that the concept speaks to modern audiences. If you want to see that man is a mixture of good and evil, just read the newspaper, watch the news, or read a book about any period of human history.

While it's true that we shouldn't dwell on the negative side of human nature, ignoring it is not only unrealistic, but dangerous. Ignoring the human capacity for evil leads us to believe that we don't need rules and guidelines for behavior for ourselves or others, when the truth is that we do. Acknowledging the dark side does not mean that most people aren't good people or that they don't want to do the right thing, but it does mean that even the best person alive is incapable of always doing what is best for himself and others. It simply means that we can't count on ourselves to make the right decisions on our own.

In making me realize all this about myself, God made me realize why my search for Him had been unsuccessful. I hadn't been able to find God because there had been no room for God in my life. There had been no room for God in my life because I had been determined to do everything on my own. I had been determined to "be like God, knowing good from evil." I had placed all my faith in myself, so it had been impossible for me to place my faith in God. You cannot be independent and dependent at the same time.

Well, now God was showing me that I was dependent. He was showing me that I couldn't do things on my own. And this is where I saw that

Christianity isn't really negative at all; in fact, it is gloriously positive. Because what Christianity offers is a way to once again close that gap between ourselves and God, and that is through faith in His Son, Jesus Christ. We can't make correct decisions for ourselves, but we can seek His will for our lives, and there we will find the correct decisions.

But there is a price to pay for this gift. What God calls for is not merely standing up in church and waving one's arms. What God calls for is full commitment. What God calls for is a giving up of the old self, leaving the old life behind like a snake sheds its skin, and being "born again" into His care.

As I lay there in that bed, sweating and shaking, I knew that it was all or nothing. To truly accept Jesus as Lord of my life, I had to leave everything behind. The old life had to end, right then and there. I had to renounce my vow to make it on my own. I had to admit defeat.

Well, I was ready to do just that. I lay on that bed and I cried out to God. I cried out for Jesus. I had never thought of myself as an addict before, but now I found myself confessing to God that I was a hopeless drug addict. I had always thought that I could quit drugs whenever I wanted, that I was in control. But now I was crying out to God that I was not in control and that I couldn't stop and that I wanted to stop but that I needed His strength because mine wasn't enough.

"I don't know what to do," I kept saying. "I need Jesus." That is all I knew to say. "I need Jesus to get me out of this." I remember saying, "God, if you would just give me Jesus, and help me turn this page in my book, I will give you the rest of my life!"

This went on for three days. When I came to, it was a Sunday, and Jesus spoke to me with the same voice as in the hotel room. He said, *"Get baptized today."* So I phoned up my friend Chester.

"Hey, how're you doing?" he asked. "We've been praying for you a lot lately. What's been going on?"

"Well, I can't tell you right now," I said, "but thing's haven't been good. But today I'm going to get baptized. The Lord told me to get baptized."

"Great!" he said. "Do you know what day it is today?"

"It's Sunday, isn't it?"

"Yes, and its Pentecost."

"What's that?" I asked. He explained that Pentecost had come after Christ's resurrection when many disciples had gathered for prayer, and the Holy Spirit had descended upon them, and from that meeting the members of the church had gone out and established the Christian faith. Well, I didn't know what he was talking about. The words "Holy Spirit" meant nothing to me.

I said, "Well, whatever day it is, I am going to church tonight and I am getting baptized." He said that was great and that they would meet me there.

When I got there, they took me into a back room where there were twelve other people also getting baptized that night. They had us put on white robes in which we were to be baptized. We were standing behind the curtains next to the organ and I could see a portion of the congregation from where I was standing—there were about 1,300 people there that night. The service was starting and the congregation was singing a hymn. The worship was interrupted by Pastor Jack, who got up and said, "It is Pentecost today and I think the Lord would have us sing in the Spirit. Let us sing the next hymn in the Spirit."

    I had no idea what it meant to sing "in the Spirit." I just assumed it was another way of saying to sing *with* spirit. But when the hymn started, I knew right away this was something different. You see, many of the people were singing in tongues, and if you've never heard people speaking or singing in tongues, it can be quite a shock. I was standing there thinking, "Hmm, very interesting. Spanish, Greek, and Klingon all at the same time."

We were still standing right behind the organ, and suddenly the organ stopped playing, but the voices of the people kept singing. And at that point, something happened to me. The only way I can describe it is to say that something opened up above me, and I went up. I wasn't hearing the church singing anymore; I was hearing the angels singing. I heard the host of heaven singing. Millions of them. I was transported into a celestial realm by what I was hearing.

Having been a musician all my life, I had an enormous record collection, and I had heard every kind of music that the planet Earth has to offer. I had heard music from China, from Russia, from India, from all parts of Africa. I had even heard Eskimo music. But what I was hearing that night was not of this Earth; it cannot be described in earthly language. What I heard that night was so perfect that the music of this Earth doesn't even come close. I can't describe it to you, but I know this much: They were singing the Song of Creation. The Song of Creation is described in Job 38:4-7 as being when the morning stars sang together and the sons of God shouted for joy. God dwells in eternity, and that song is still going on. And that night, God privileged me to hear it.

I had never heard anything so perfect in my life. It was devastating. I wept. Later, I asked my friend Chester, "How long were you guys singing when you were singing in the Spirit?" He replied, "Three or four minutes." But what I heard went on for hours and hours and hours. I had been caught up into eternity.

In Second Corinthians 12:2-4, the Apostle Paul describes getting caught up into the Third Heaven. To tell you the truth, I don't know if I was caught up into the first, the second, the third, or the ninth heaven. I didn't even know how many heavens there were, but I knew that I was caught up into one of them.

And when the music stopped, I couldn't wait to get into the water and be baptized. Well, of course, it turned out I was stuck at the back of the line, so I had to wait for twelve other people to get baptized. That takes a long time, and I was growing more and more impatient. I wanted so badly to get into that water to be cleansed of my past life. So, while these other twelve people had tiptoed very lightly into the water to avoid making a splash, this poor fool just graciously fell in. I wanted in so badly, I couldn't wait.

So I was finally in the water, and they dunked me under, and when they pulled me out, I want you to know that I came out brand, spanking new. I was delivered from seventeen years of drugs, right there in the water. Not everybody gets delivered like that, but that is what Jesus did for me. I went into that water an addict, and I came out clean.

When I got out and stood in the back and began drying off with a towel, I started tapping my side. I couldn't see anything unusual, but I had this strange feeling that there was this hole in my side. I mean a hole about a foot wide, and I kept tapping my side where I felt it and looking down to see where the hole was. I couldn't see it with my eyes, but I could feel my hand passing through it! I kept looking back into the water, because I knew that something had been taken out of me and left in the water. I wouldn't know for a while what it was.

I went home and told my roommate that I was out of the drug business and that I was never taking drugs again. I went down the next day and applied for unemployment to tide me over until I could get my life straight and get a job. I knew I was in for a period of bad withdrawals from my drug habit, and I knew I couldn't hold a job during what I was about to go through. For the next week or two I just sat in that house reading the Bible, waiting for the withdrawals to begin. I had been a drug addict for seventeen years—I knew I was in for some difficult times, but I had faith that God would give me the strength to get through it.

Day after day I sat there reading the Bible and just waiting. I would look at my watch and think, "Well, any minute I'm going to start shaking and sweating. Any minute the craving is going to start, the anxiety, the paranoia, the nausea, the dry heaves." And I sat there and waited, and it never came. There was no anxiety, just peace. There were no shakes and sweats; I just kept reading my Bible. To this day I have never had the slightest symptom of withdrawal after being addicted for more than seventeen years. That's unheard of.

I figured it out later. You remember those three days when I was lying in bed sweating and shaking and thinking I was going to die? God had the grace to let me suffer that way because He knew it was the only way to make me realize how much I needed Him. And when I gave my life to Him, He had the grace to take away my addiction in one clean sweep. He knew that I had already suffered enough—His purpose had been fulfilled.

You see, that's what God took out of me in the water. He took away my addiction. I had been a drug addict for seventeen years, and I came out of that water clean. It ended right then and there. God took it out of me—He took out of my side the demon that had been tempting me, and I have never since been tempted by drugs. Jesus answered my prayer, and turned that page in my life, and that chapter was over. Period.

Just before this, Bruce Johnston of The Beach Boys had asked me if I wanted to play with them on tour. I had played with Elton John and Hall & Oates, and now I had the chance to be a Beach Boy, at least for one tour. I had accepted, and Bruce had sent me a videotape of one of their shows so I could start learning the tunes. When I got baptized, I had to call Bruce and ask him to find someone else. My life had changed, and I knew that I was out of rock & roll forever.

And that is how I got saved. But that was really just the beginning of what God had planned for my life. When we get saved, no matter how dramatic it is, it is not the end of the story. It is only the beginning.

Chapter Nine

A New Life

So there I was, a Christian, delivered by the grace of Jesus Christ from seventeen years of drug addiction, and I was living in a house where people came to get their drugs. So what did I do? Why, I started witnessing, of course. These poor junkies would come to the door, and I would welcome them with a smile. Thinking I was the same old Caleb, they would come in for a chat and a toke or two, but when they walked inside, I could see them looking around at how the house had been cleaned up. Then they would look at me and see that I was cleaned up, too—relaxed, smiling, alert.

"Boy, you look great," they would say.

"What's happened to you?"

"Come on in and I'll tell you," I would say. We would sit down in the den, and between us would be the little table with the lazy Susan on top that we had always used to deal out the drugs. Now the only thing on that table was a Bible. (I still have that table—I call it my "Sanctified Lazy Susan.") They knew something was up right away, and it was sort of fun seeing how long it took each one to realize that this old cokehead, Caleb Quaye, was seriously sharing with them the Gospel of Jesus Christ.

I would just start telling them what had happened to me and how drugs had helped destroy my life and how there was a way for them to make sure it didn't destroy theirs. In the past, these guys had always had time to smoke a joint and talk aimlessly about the deeper mysteries of the universe. But now, truly confronted with those mysteries and having them explained for the first time, they couldn't wait to get out of there. They would start fidgeting and sweating, then they would remember some urgent business they had to attend to. Only God knows if I planted any seeds that eventually found soil—I was sharing out of the pure joy that Christ had brought to my life.

Needless to say, my roommate and former business partner wasn't very happy about my new sales technique. After a week or two, I moved in with my friend Chester Thompson until I could find a place of my own. A couple of weeks later, I found an apartment in Van Nuys, right across the street from The Church on the Way. I could walk right across the street to go to church. This was still very soon after my baptism and I was still on welfare, so I would go over to the pastor's office during the day looking for discipleship. I didn't need to go to church every time the doors opened—I was already there when they opened!

By this time I had filed for divorce. I had not gotten over the sense of hurt and betrayal I felt at the breakup, but as a new Christian, the Holy Spirit convicted me that I needed to do all I could to try to save my marriage. I went to Patricia and acknowledged that I had not been a very good husband or father, and I apologized for any hurt or damage I may have caused her. She seemed glad that I had changed my direction in life, but as far as us getting back together, she had no interest. It wasn't long after our divorce that she married Bill Quateman.

When it became clear that God had spared me the debilitating effects of drug withdrawals, I knew I had to find a job. My best friend in the church at that time (and to this day) was Pee Wee Hill, who played bass in the church's praise band. Back then Pee Wee was painting houses for a living, and he was able to get me a job with the same company.

During those early months, I was completely anonymous within the church. No one knew my background. No one even knew that I played guitar. You cannot imagine how strange all this was to me. From the age of fifteen, I had hobnobbed with some of the biggest names in the music industry. I had fronted a band that had played to huge rock festivals in Europe. I had played before sold-out stadiums with two of the hottest acts of the '70s. I had been recognized on the streets of England and America. And through it all, I had been part of a close-knit music community that is like its own little secret society spread all around the world. I was known to every band and welcomed into every studio in the world.

In fact, I was still ranked as one of the top guitarists in the world. If I wanted to, I could pick up the telephone and call the top rock stars and producers in the world, as well as a handful of other celebrities. And yet here I was, putting on white overalls and showing up to paint houses all over

Los Angeles. There were undoubtedly times when fellow rock stars or music industry executives drove right by a house I was painting. How surprised they would have been had they looked closely! It was very strange, but then, they do say that God works in mysterious ways.

I would like to be able to say that I found new peace in my introduction to manual labor. In reality, I hated the work, but I understood that God was humbling me. I understood that He was taking me through a major transition in my life, and that this transition required Him to take me as far away from my old lifestyle as was possible. Slaving away as an anonymous house painter was certainly a long way from playing guitar in front of huge crowds and hanging out with some of the most famous people in the world. In stark contrast to my previous career, this was really work!

The job did bring some much-needed structure to my life. I had never had a real job before. I had never had to clock in, to get a certain amount of work done, to come back from my breaks at a certain time, to take orders. I needed the discipline, and I certainly needed a sense of order in my life. I didn't fully realize it at the time, and I didn't like it, but God knew what He was doing.

The job also gave me lots of time to think, and lots of quiet to do it in. That's what I needed most, and again, God knew it. At lunchtime I would go alone to whatever fast food place was nearby and sit and read my Bible for an hour. I hadn't been much of a scholar since taking up guitar, but now I loved the feeling of wisdom flowing into my brain and the knowledge of God flowing into my heart.

    The transition God was taking me through was a paradigm shift on every level. I was leaving behind the drugs, the drinking, the sex, the fame, the money. I was leaving behind my chosen profession. I was leaving behind a lifestyle of late nights and few responsibilities. I was leaving behind my lifelong friends and acquaintances and meeting dozens of new people in the church, people whose lives were unlike those of anyone I had ever met. In a way, becoming a Christian is like moving to a new country, a country with its own vocabulary, its own culture, and its own standard of behavior. It's simply hard to imagine how God could have changed my life in a more fundamental way than He did during this period.

Soon after I joined The Church on the Way, I became part of one of their home groups. These weekly Bible studies, which met throughout the city, were an important source of fellowship and friendship. In one of my first meetings, I shared all that had happened to me. Afterward, the youth pastor, Dr. Ralph Torres, said, "Caleb, I'd like to see you in my office on Monday." Ralph offered himself as my counselor. He provided me with the discipleship and accountability I desperately needed. Ralph became my mentor and friend, beginning a personal and professional relationship that continues to this day.

One way that Ralph reached the young

people of the community was through a series of concerts by Christian musicians. In September 1982, Ralph brought in Ken Medema, a blind fellow who was a piano player and a great testifier. I was still a very new Christian, and everyone kept telling me I should go hear this guy. Chester and his wife and I got there just as Ralph was leading Ken onto the stage. Ken played some great music, and between songs he would talk about his relationship with Jesus. It was obvious that the Spirit of the Lord was heavy in the place. Ken was the first person I had ever heard who used his music as a way to reach people for Christ. I started to feel convicted, and before I knew it, I heard the voice again.

"Caleb, you see what this guy is doing?" the

Lord said. *"I want you to do this for me."* When the concert ended, I went with Chester and his wife out into the foyer so they could get some of Ken's tapes. I was standing there in sort of a daze trying to digest what God had just told me. All of a sudden, Ralph rushed up to me out of breath—he had run all the way from the stage. He stuck his finger in my face and said, "God just told me that you are to play at the next concert in November. Will you do it?" God had said the same thing to Ralph He had said to me. What could I say?

"Yeah, sure," I said. "I'll be glad to."

But on my way home, I had a little chat with the Lord. "Uh, Lord, I don't know any Christian music. I don't have a band. What am I supposed to do?" Well, over the next week, I wrote thirteen brand-new songs. They just poured out of me, my soul rejoicing in what God was doing in my life. My friend Pee Wee Hill was a bass player, so he and I put together a band with some other members of the church. We did the concert in November, and twenty-five people got saved. As I watched these people come to the front of the church to give themselves to Christ, I realized what God had in mind for me.

The Caleb Quaye Band stayed together for five years. We would play my songs, and in between I would give my testimony or do a little preaching. Even though we were singing praise songs, I was still playing my style of music, a sort of toned down rock and jazz fusion. I called it Good News Music. Audiences loved us and we were soon brought to the attention of the Christian record companies, but the same old problem arose. They were afraid to sign a deal with us because they couldn't pigeonhole us in any existing category. That was okay, though, because this band wasn't about making records—it was about sharing the gospel of Jesus Christ with our live audiences.

We played all over Los Angeles in churches and community centers. When the Olympics were held in L.A. in 1984, we teamed with Y.W.A.M. (Youth With A Mission) and played in parks and bars all over the city. There was a ministry for homeless and street people called Oasis, and we would play in their mission house on a regular basis. We even played one time at a church youth outreach that was held at a Chuck E. Cheese's.

From Madison Square Garden to Chuck E. Cheese's! At that point I could honestly say that I had done it all.

Did I see this as a comedown in my career? Not at all. During the five years that our band played together, we saw a couple of thousand people come to Christ. It had been fun to play at Madison Square Garden in the old days, but now I was having fun *and* doing something truly important. Now the people around me were real people, not celebrities and hangers on. Now when I played my music, my eyes were clear and my heart was light. When I finished, I went home to my own home and my own bed. And it wasn't long before God blessed me with someone to go home to.

The very first night I had gone to that home

group back in 1983, there was a girl there named Lydia, who was also friends with Pee Wee and his wife Michiko. I had my mind on other things at that stage, so I didn't particularly notice Lydia when I first met her, but as I got to know her, I was drawn to her sweet temperament. She is what you would describe as a "pure heart." She's very innocent, which is nothing short of a miracle given her background. She shared her testimony with the group, and as I heard it, I developed a real respect for her.

She had never known her father. Her mom was born in Puerto Rico and was uneducated, and she came over to escape the unrest that followed the Cuban revolution. Lydia was raised in a very rough neighborhood in Spanish Harlem in Manhattan.

Her mom slept around, took drugs, and verbally and emotionally abused Lydia and her sister. It's amazing that both the girls didn't end up hooked on drugs and walking the streets. Lydia's spirit rebelled against all that, and she was determined to get an education, so she worked her way through a secretarial school in Connecticut. She got secretarial jobs in Manhattan and began to move up in pay and respect. While she worked, she went back to school and got her education degree so she could become a teacher. She worked her way out of the ghetto.

In her early twenties, she drank and partied along with her friends, but with her mother's drug abuse, she was wary of going in that direction. Like me, she found herself looking for answers. During her lunch hours, she would stop by a Catholic church near her office in Manhattan and just sit there enjoying the peace.

She got married to a man who worked in the film industry, so they moved out to California. While she was married, her sister, who is also an educator, became a Christian, and she started witnessing to Lydia. One Sunday, Lydia walked into a Baptist church and accepted the Lord. Unfortunately, her husband wanted no part of her new-found faith, and this caused some tension in the marriage. Then one night she caught him having an affair.

When we met, we were both in the final stages of divorce, so we were able to offer support and encouragement to each other. A friendship developed, and I found myself looking forward to seeing her. After some time had passed, God spoke to me again.

I was house-sitting for Chester Thompson while he and his wife were out of town. He lent me his car because I didn't have one. As I was driving along, I suddenly heard God say to me, *"It's time for you to go talk to Lydia, because I've given her to you for a wife."* I nearly wrecked Chester's car. Lydia and I had really known each other for only about six months.

I waited four or five days, thinking that God might change His mind, but I remained convicted that He meant Lydia to be my wife. Finally, I called her up.

"We need to talk," I said somewhat

brusquely.

"About what?" she asked.

"About us."

"Okay," she said, slightly surprised. "Why don't you come over for dinner?" After dinner she put her daughter to bed while I waited very nervously in the living room. When she finally sat down so that we could talk, I went into what I call "prophetic overdrive." All these thoughts and feelings just poured out.

"I'm-living-for-God-now-and-I-want-to-do-whatever-God-wants-and-I-think-he-may-be-calling-me-to-the-ministry-and-it-seems-that-you're-supposed-to-be-my-wife-so-what-do-you-say?" When I finished, Lydia looked at me like she was a little bit in shock. In describing it later, she said, "It was all kind of nice, but there was nothing in it about actually being in love with me." I knew I had made the most disastrous proposal ever, so you can imagine my relief when she said, "Yes." She explained to me that she also had feelings for me, but that she had been trying to ignore them because of her recent divorce. In fact, she had gone home to New York three separate times because she couldn't see me while she processed her feelings for me.

We dated for six months. Lydia had a four-year-old daughter named Melissa from her earlier marriage, whom I grew to love as my own. My daughter, Lucy, was six at that time, and although she lived with her mother, I brought her to church with me every Sunday. She and Melissa quickly formed a strong friendship. On April 7, 1984, Lydia and I were married with both our daughters as part of the ceremony. That summer, Lucy and Melissa both asked if they could be baptized. I discussed it with Lucy's mother, and I was happy that she not only agreed, but she even came to the baptismal service. Three years later, on June 26, 1987, Lydia and I were blessed with a daughter of our own, Stephanie.

You have to understand how different my new married relationship was for me. I was used to getting women whenever I wanted them with absolutely no commitment attached. My relationship with my first wife had just happened, and I had put virtually no effort into it. Now, for the first time, I had to learn what it meant to be a husband and a father. The feminists all believe that

Christian men just want to subjugate women, but it wasn't until I became a Christian that I ever made a conscious effort to treat women with respect.

When I started dating Lydia, I had been painting houses for about six months and, as I said, I really hated it. Once we got engaged, I started looking for something more permanent. Someone in the church got me a job working in the warehouse and driving a truck for Sparrow Records, a Christian record company in Chatsworth. My boss there was a seventeen-year-old kid, so I got another dose of that discipline that God was teaching me.

In June 1984, my friend Ralph Torres left The Church on the Way to start a church in Pasadena. In January 1985, Lydia and I moved with him to help in this effort. The church we helped set up was Pasadena Foursquare, part of the International Church of the Foursquare Gospel, a Pentecostal denomination headquartered in Los Angeles with 1,700 churches in America and 18,000 worldwide. Foursquare takes its name from the four cardinal points of Christian doctrine: We take Jesus to be the Savior, Healer, Baptizer, and the Coming King.

It was impractical to commute from Pasadena to Chatsworth, so I began looking for different work. A guy in our church was leaving his job in the print shop at Fuller Seminary in Pasadena, so he referred me to the proper people. I explained to the man who interviewed me that I had never done this type of work before. "You know what?"

he asked. "I've interviewed three other people who had better qualifications, but I feel I'm supposed to give this job to you." I stayed there for two and a half years and ended up as manager.

In 1985, I received a telephone call from one of Elton John's attorneys. He explained to me that Elton and Bernie Taupin were suing Dick James for some back royalties they felt they were owed from foreign sales. They were also contesting the original contract—the one signed as a result of The Great Purge—claiming that it had been unfair and had been signed under "undue influence." The lawsuit was not merely asking for more money, but for the return of the copyrights to every song produced throughout their six-year contract with James.

The attorney explained that, because I had been intimately involved in the process that led to Elton's and Bernie's original contract, I was the only one who could answer certain questions. Would I be willing to come to England to testify in the trial?

I met with the attorney in Los Angeles at Connie Hillman's office, the West Coast branch of Elton's management. He explained things in greater detail and made arrangements to fly me to England. It was strange being back in London, and even stranger to be walking into the Old Bailey, England's central courthouse.

When it was my turn, I stepped up into the dock, the British version of the witness stand. (In American courtrooms you sit down when testifying, but in England you stand up.) Before I was asked the first question concerning the suit, the judge, in the haughty, nasal twang peculiar to the upper class British, asked me about my occupation.

"Mr. Quaye, it says here you are a minister. Do you have a parish?"

"Well, kind of," I said, not sure if he knew the difference between the Protestant evangelical denominations and the high church in England.

"Well," he said, "what is Foursquare?"

"Well," I said, "it's a Pentecostal denomination. We take Jesus Christ to be the Savior, Healer, Baptizer, and the Coming King." The silence in that courtroom was amazing. I couldn't believe that I had been able to present Jesus to the proceedings.

"Oh," said the judge, still in his haughty

nasal accent. "Oh, really? Well, very good, then." I was cracking up inside and praising God at the same time.

I remember looking down at Dick and Stephen James, and Dick looked up and smiled at me just as he would have had we run into each other on the street. I certainly had no intention of harming Dick James, and as far as I know, my testimony didn't. The prosecutor kept trying to get me to say something damaging to him, asking my personal opinion of him and other things that really had nothing to do with the facts of the case. I wouldn't let them do that. I told them flat out that I had nothing against this man. Simply put, I said, Dick was a good man. Yes, he drove a hard bargain and got a piece of the action whenever he could, but what's wrong with that? In my opinion, he wasn't out to harm anyone or to rip them off.

I only testified for a couple of hours that one afternoon, then went back to California the next day. The trial ended a month or so later with something of a split decision. The original contract was upheld and Dick James Music retained copyright to the songs for its duration. However, it was ruled that DJM's method of calculating foreign royalties had deprived Elton of his full share, so DJM was ordered to pay him the difference, an amount that I am told ended up being less than a million British pounds. Both sides claimed victory after the trial, but I was torn between my friendship with Elton and my respect for Dick James, who had given us our first shot in the music industry.

It was during the trial that I first told Elton about my Christianity. At the trial, he told me he was recording an album at the studio called The Mill, and he invited me over. He sent a limo over to my hotel, and for the first time in ten years I walked into an Elton John recording session. He was recording an album called *Ice on Fire*. It was old home week for me, as I got to see Gus Dudgeon, Steve Brown, Davey Johnstone, and the others for the first time since 1976. It was great talking about the old days with them.

Elton kept asking me, "What's happened to you? You look great!" When I told him, I could tell that he was uncomfortable, and things got a little weird between us. It's never my intent to push my spiritual beliefs on others, so I played it as cool as possible, but I could tell that he had a problem with my new-found faith. "Well, I believe in the *human spirit*," he would say. He told me some story about how he had been in Jamaica and someone had gotten sick, and they took this fellow into the ocean and chanted some voodoo chant, and apparently the guy got better, so he saw it as a triumph of the human spirit.

He took me into the control room where Gus Dudgeon was sitting. "Play this track for Caleb," he said. Gus played it, and Elton reached over and turned the volume way up. I don't remember the name of the song, but I know it didn't end up on the album. All I remember was that it was something about God and the devil having a fight, and the devil wins in the end. Elton was going, "Hear that?

This is where the devil wins!" I'm thinking, "What is going on here?"

After that, though, he softened, and the recording session continued. I stayed for three or four hours. The next day, before I left to fly back home, he called me at the hotel and asked me if there was anything he could do for me. He asked more than once, so I said, "Well, our church needs a new sound system."

"How much do you need?" he asked. "Would $5,000 be enough?" Sure enough, not long after I arrived home, a check for $5,000 arrived through Elton's management for our new sound system. As is usually the case with Elton, his good side showed through in the end.

He also told me that he would be playing at

the Universal Amphitheatre in L.A. on his upcoming tour. He invited me to come join them backstage at the concert, then added, "Bring your guitar." So on the day of the concert, I took my Fender Stratocaster and hung out backstage with the band. At the end of the show, when the band went back out for an encore, Elton had me come out with them. Elton introduced me as a "special guest," and when he announced my name, the crowd roared. With no practice or preparation, I joined in on four songs I hadn't played in ten years. I had to keep looking at Davey to try to figure out which key we were in, but the audience didn't seem to notice, and we all had a lot of fun.

While in England for the trial, I was also able to visit my mother for the first time in several years. She been over to the States several times since we had moved there, and during those visits, as well as in our telephone conversations, I would naturally raise the topic of her spiritual life. She had been raised a devout Catholic but had long ago fallen away from the church. Whenever I would bring up the subject, she was always very polite, but that's as far as it went.

The year after the trial, she came over to the States again. We took her to a service at The Church on the Way, and they served communion. My mother took communion, which you're not supposed to do unless you believe in the deity of Jesus Christ. As we were leaving, I told my wife, "We've got to do something. She's not a Christian and she's taking communion. You've got to talk to her."

The next day, I got a call at work from Lydia.

"Guess what happened?" she asked.

"I don't know," I said. "What?"

"Your mother just accepted Jesus Christ as her Savior."

"What? How did that happen?"

"We were just sitting having coffee, and the subject came up, and I led her to the Lord."

Well, I was ecstatic. My mum had found Jesus at the age of sixty-seven. But when I got home that night, I just had to ask her something.

"Mum," I said, "I've been talking to you about Jesus for several years. What made you pick today?"

"Well," she said, "I knew you had received Jesus, but I wasn't going to do it just for you. I had to do it for myself."

When you're helping to start a church, you have to wear many hats. Naturally, I was the one who helped organize the worship services. I gave my testimony several times, just as I had at The Church on the Way, but by now I was familiar enough with Scripture to begin expanding my story by weaving in biblical messages. Before long, I was actually preaching sermons on an occasional basis and leading the worship service on a regular basis. In addition to playing at other churches with The Caleb Quaye Band, I was invited to preach at other churches, as well. Eventually, I began to receive offers for ministerial staff positions.

Caleb Quaye, the old coke-head, a minister? Never in a million years would I have dreamed that such a turn of events would occur! Yet the whole transition had occurred so smoothly, and God had taught me so much about His Word and His plan for me and for the world, that it seemed the natural thing to do. I went to Pastor Torres and told him that I thought it was time for me to go full-time into the ministry. In January 1988, I became the associate pastor and staff evangelist of Pasadena Foursquare.

Unfortunately, this meant the end of The Caleb Quaye Band, because now all my efforts had to be focused on the church's praise band. While it was impractical to take that band all around L.A. as we did with the old band, we nonetheless used it for evangelical outreach. For example, our church is very near the Rose Bowl Parade route, so we started doing an outreach there on New Year's Day. Our first year there, a fight broke out and a policeman was getting beaten up by some drunk guys, and we ran down and saved him. Maybe that's why we were the only church that the city would grant a permit to play at this event, an event that gave us an audience of nearly half a million people in a single day.

    My time spent as a worship leader and associate pastor on the staff of the Pasadena Foursquare Church turned out to be an invaluable, on-the-job-training school of ministry. You see, I had never gone to Bible college or seminary. Instead, I learned through the mentoring of my dear friend and pastor, Rev. Ralph Torres, to whom I am forever grateful. Under his direction, I was literally learning something new every day about the wonders of the love of God. My abilities and my reputation as a worship leader built over time. I began to settle into my new life, and I began to feel at home in the Christian community. The darkness of my former life was fading away as if it had never happened.

Then, out of the blue, my father called again.

Chapter Ten

Reunited

I hadn't spoken to my father since that night in March 1974, right before I left England to move to Chicago. I had been on the road throughout the rest of the '70s, then I had gone through the process of becoming a Christian, and my past life by that time seemed like a bad dream that I wanted only to forget. Needless to say, my father represented that past life, not just because of the abusive behavior I witnessed as a child, but also because of the weird relationship we had when I was taking drugs with him as an adult. In all the years since, I had hardly thought about my father.

Before I remarried in 1984, Lydia and I

attended a premarital counseling class at our church. The pastor teaching the class said, "There are some things from your past that you should take into your marriage, but there are other things from your past that you should not take into your marriage. You cannot be free to love someone fully if you are carrying around hatred for someone else, or shame about past deeds, or insecurities caused by childhood factors. These things should be given over to God and resolved before you get married." He specifically talked about our having unresolved issues with our parents. I'd never thought about this before, but as he spoke, I began to feel very much under conviction. I began to realize that my relationship with my father was very much unresolved and that I still felt a great deal of anger toward him.

"What we're going to do," said our instructor, "is pray individually. We're going to acknowledge these unresolved issues in our lives and turn them over to God. For some of you, there are even situations from the past that you've forgotten about, but that are still affecting you. You need to ask the Holy Spirit to help you remember those things and turn them over to God." I knew in my heart that I needed to do exactly what he said.

We turned around and knelt over our chairs, and I began praying very earnestly about my father—the pain he had caused in our household and the sense of abandonment with which he had left me at such a young age. As I knelt and prayed, I tried to name as many specifics as I could and forgive my father for each one.

"Lord, I forgive my father for throwing my grandmother down the stairs.

"Lord, I forgive my father for getting drunk and beating my mother and sisters.   "Lord, I forgive my father for putting the family in the car and driving through every stoplight in town at full speed.

"Lord, I forgive my father for refusing to teach me how to play guitar.

"Lord, I forgive my father for leaving me when I was twelve."

I left each of those things there with Jesus, and when I got up off my knees, I felt a hundred pounds lighter.

In 1985, three years after I had been saved, I

woke up one morning with a strong impression that the Lord wanted me to write my dad a letter. I called my sister in England and got his address in Amsterdam, where he was then living with a new wife. I wrote him a two-page letter telling him what I was doing and that I had become a Christian. In this letter, I told him that I had forgiven him for everything he had done to me and to the family. I didn't expect a reply, and I didn't get one. But, again, I felt better just having taken the step to resolve those issues and turn them over to God.

Nine years went by. It was 1994, twenty years after my last conversation with my father— the conversation in which I had asked him if he believed in life after death. I was now the associate pastor of Pasadena Foursquare Church, and I was in my office one day when my secretary said, "Caleb, there's some fellow on the phone here from Amsterdam." I couldn't think of anyone I knew in Amsterdam, and to show you how much my life had changed, I was trying to think of another pastor I knew who might be doing missions work or interim preaching in Amsterdam.

"Hi, Caleb," said the voice on the phone. "It's me. It's your dad."

"Wow," I said. "This is a surprise. What's going on?"

"Well, I'm just calling to ask your advice," he said. This was an even bigger surprise. My dad—this man who had ruled our household with an iron fist—asking me for advice? "I got your letter and I know what you're doing," he said. "And I need your advice."

"Advice about what?" I asked.

"Caleb, I've got cancer."

Immediately, the Holy Spirit instructed me to start witnessing to him. I didn't ask what kind of cancer he had or when he had found out or what the prognosis was—I just started presenting the Gospel of Jesus Christ to him.

"Have you got a Bible?" I asked.

"Yes, I do," he said. Once again I was surprised. But he went and got his Bible, and we started reading Scripture together. As we did, I became overcome with emotion and started crying. But I continued to lead him through the Scripture, showing him how we stood condemned by our sin, but how Jesus Christ took our sins upon Himself and died so that we might be washed clean by His blood, and that all we had to do to receive eternal forgiveness was to believe that He had done this for us and to accept Him as our Savior and as the Lord of our lives. And right there on the phone, in our first conversation in twenty years, I led my father to Jesus.

It was only then that I got the details of his sickness. He had been diagnosed with throat cancer and was scheduled to begin chemotherapy the following week. I told him that I and my church would be praying for him. Every day for the next week, I, my family, the church staff, and the entire congregation prayed fervently that my father might be healed of his cancer. Perhaps more importantly, we thanked God that he had seen fit to bring my father to salvation.

A week later he called me back.

"I've got good news," he said.

"What's that?"

"I went in there and they took another set of X-rays, and it turns out that the cancer had stopped spreading."

"Praise God," I said.

"Yes," he replied. "They said that they thought they could get all the cancer out with surgery."

The surgery lasted eleven hours. It included taking out part of his tongue and other parts of his mouth, replacing what they could with skin grafts. It was very risky surgery because of all the anesthesia and other drugs they had to give him. He later told me that he knew he was in danger, and he began praying, "Jesus, if I'm going to die, all I ask is the opportunity to go see my son one more time before I go."

They were able to remove all the cancer, and my father recovered fully, although missing a portion of his tongue and gums. When he was sufficiently healed, his wife's family pooled the money and bought him an airplane ticket to Los Angeles. In August 1994, I went to LAX and watched with joy in my heart as my father—now smaller and older than ever, but also now a brother in Christ—was wheeled off the plane in a wheelchair. I bent down, and for the first time in our lives, we hugged.

Our relationship now grew as wonderful as

it had previously been strange. He stayed with us an entire month, and during that time he and I were fully reconciled. For the first time in my life, I really got to know my dad. We would sit out on the porch talking until three o'clock in the morning, my father struggling to pronounce his words correctly with part of his tongue missing. He would tell me stories about his childhood I'd never heard, stories about his abusive stepfather and alcoholic mother, and I began to understand why he had turned out the way he had.

I learned that he had long been carrying a heavy burden of guilt for what he had done to our family. He would sit on the couch and watch my family and my children, and tears would well up in his eyes. "Caleb," he would say, "if I could have had half of what you have here, my life would have been so different. But I didn't know how." I realized for the first time that my father really wasn't to blame for much of what he had done—he had merely treated his family the way he had been treated as a child. Watching him recognize what he had missed in life made me appreciate all the more the things that I had almost missed, as well.

During that month, he went on vacation with us up to a mountain resort called Big Bear. While we were there, I learned that he had never been baptized. My youngest daughter was planning to be baptized by me when we got back home, so I asked my father if I could have the privilege of baptizing him. The following Sunday, I baptized my daughter and my father, and what a blessing it was seeing him come out of the water clean and renewed just as I had been nearly fifteen years before. The abuse and abandonment and frustration of my childhood was behind me now, because the man who had caused it all was now dead—he had been reborn as a new creature in Jesus Christ.

But that wasn't all God was doing in my life. The day we got back from vacation, I received a letter from the leadership of my denomination asking me if I felt led to serve as the national music and worship director. Because the headquarters of the International Church of the Foursquare Gospel are located in Los Angeles, I had gotten to know many of the staff there, and they had all heard me play and preach at various events. Not only was it an honor to serve my denomination in this new capacity, it also meant that I would get to visit and play at Foursquare churches throughout the nation.

My father was proud of me for that, and as excited as I was that God was allowing me to use my musical abilities to do His work. Was it just coincidence that this letter arrived while my father was visiting me, or was that all part of God's plan to reconcile us fully, put the past behind us, and draw us closer to each other and to Him?

I didn't see my father again for six years, but we stayed in touch by telephone and letter. The past was all put behind us, and he often expressed how proud he was of what I was doing. He would ask questions about the Bible that led to many long conversations about theological questions. He was too weak to go to church, but he loved the Lord and he was always reading his Bible. How wonderful for me to be able to encourage him in his faith during this time!

One day in 1998, I got a surprise phone call from my old bandmate, Roger Pope.

"Do you have a brother?" he asked.

"Not that I know of," I replied.

"Well, there's this singer on television named Finley Quaye who looks just like you."

I said, "Well, this is news to me." So I called my dad, and he said, "Yes, we're checking it out." On Christmas Eve, 1998, my father called me back and said, "Remember how you always wanted a brother?"

"Yes?"

"Well, you've got one. He's standing right

here." My father handed the telephone to Finley, and we talked for the first time.

It turned out that back in 1973, my father had a one-night stand with a woman in northern England shortly after leaving his second wife. He had no idea that he had produced a child from that encounter, but Finley's mother had always told him who his father was. When Finley was about twelve years old, his mother had died, reportedly of a heroin addiction. He had been raised by a series of aunts of uncles. Somewhere in his teens, Finley had decided to go into music, although I don't know how much of that was a result of the Quaye genes and how much was a desire to follow in the footsteps of his absentee father. In any case, in 1998 he released his first album, *Maverick a Strike,* which went platinum in Europe. The resulting television appearances led to his meeting with my—I mean, our—father.

Finley and my father were reconciled. In March 1999, Finley came to America to play some promotional dates. In Los Angeles, he was scheduled to play a brief promotional concert at the Virgin Records Superstore on Sunset Boulevard. He called me and invited me to come join him with my guitar. It turned out to be a lot of fun. I didn't know any of his songs, but I jumped right in and jammed with the band.

"Boy, you really know how to play that thing," Finley said. He even told me that years before he had tracked down copies of the old Hookfoot albums.

That Sunday, he came to my church, and while he was there, he accepted an invitation to invite Christ into his heart. It was an amazing moment from my perspective, because he does look a lot like me, and here he was weeping and bawling just like I had years ago when I had raised my hand back at The Church on the Way. I ran up and gave him a big hug, and he came home with us for lunch that day, which was a joyous occasion.

In November 1999, I was invited to speak to some Foursquare churches in Holland, which gave me the opportunity to visit my father for several days. I could tell then that he was not going to last much longer, and the Lord was gracious to give me that time to say goodbye to him. The most special moments of that visit were when I would sit and play music for him. He loved to sit and listen while I played the piano—he even made a little cassette recording of me playing, and he later told me he played it every day. For me, it was like being able to return a portion of a gift to the one who had given it to me.

That was the last time I ever saw him. On March 13, 2000, while I was preaching at a church in Port Angeles, Washington, I got a telephone call from my wife telling me that my father had passed away. When I hung up, I just sat for awhile. I expected tears, but instead I heard the Lord tell me, *"It's time to celebrate. He's out of pain. He's reunited with his family, with the father he never knew. It's time to celebrate."* So I called up room service and ordered steak and lobster, and I sat in that hotel room and celebrated the grace of salvation that had cleansed my father's life and broken the chain of sin that had threatened to continue from one generation to another.

I was later told that, on his deathbed, he had forgiven everyone in his life and asked forgiveness of everyone in his life. Then he asked his wife to invite some of his friends in. After they gathered around his bed, he tried to lift his head and speak, but no sound would come out. After a few moments they realized that he wasn't trying to speak—he was trying to sing to them, but he was too weak. His lips were moving, but there was no sound. His friends looked at each other, and because he couldn't sing to them, they started singing to him. As soon as they did, my father smiled and laid his head down to rest. While they were singing to him, he passed away.

And now my father has the strength to sing again. He's in heaven, singing robust praises to the Lord. I pray that my grandfather is with him, singing along. Someday I will join them, as will Finley, my mother, my wife and daughters, and so many others in our family, and the Quaye family will join that celestial chorus that I heard the day that I was baptized with the Holy Spirit.

Over a period of three generations, Satan had tried to take one of God's most glorious creations—music— and turn it into a weapon to destroy our family. He had nearly succeeded. But the grace of God is too strong, and the gates of hell shall not prevail against it. The chain was broken, the demon cast into the pit. And today, whether on earth or in heaven, the Quaye family uses music as it was intended: to glorify and give testament to the overflowing love and grace of our Lord Jesus Christ.

Chapter Eleven

On the Road Again

So there I was, back out on the road, visiting Foursquare churches throughout the nation and even in other countries. As National Director of Worship & Music, it became my job to assist each church in its overall worship program. At every church I visited, I always had it arranged to play for the youth group. Because of my background in rock music, I knew they would listen to me when they might not listen to others.

One weekend I was in Gresham, Oregon ministering at Easthill Foursquare Church. I was staying in the home of the worship pastor, Darrell Dahlman, with whom I had been friends for several years. We were sitting and talking on a Saturday afternoon when the phone rang. Darrell handed me the phone and said, "It's for you. It's CBS News." I just assumed that the church had sent a press release to the local television station, and that they wanted to do a brief story on my visit.

The lady on the other end of the line said, "Is this Caleb Quaye?"

"Yes," I responded.

"We hear that you're the best guitar player in the world."

"Oh, really?" I asked with a chuckle. "Who says?"

"Eric Clapton said so on the David Letterman show last night."

In case there's anyone out there who doesn't

know, Eric Clapton is widely considered to be one of the premier guitar players of the rock era, with many ranking him at the top. His career began in the early '60s with groups like The Yardbirds, Cream, and Blind Faith. His solo career, which began in the early '70s, continued to flourish until he announced his retirement in 2016.

Clapton's biggest hits include the 1972 classic "Layla," his 1974 remake of Bob Marley's "I Shot the Sheriff" (which went to number one and introduced reggae to the popular market in America), 1978's "Wonderful Tonight," and 1992's "Tears in Heaven," written in memory of his four-year-old son Conor, who had tragically fallen to his death from the window of a New York apartment. His 1992 "Unplugged" album and his 1994 "From the Cradle," an album of old blues tunes, both went to Number One on the American charts.

It turned out that the lady on the phone was with CBS News in Portland, Oregon. To this day I don't know how they tracked me down. I asked her to tell me exactly what Eric Clapton had said. She said that Letterman had asked him, "So what's it like to be the best guitar player in the world?", and Eric replied, "I'm not. Caleb Quaye is." I was flabbergasted.

During my brief stint with Bluesology in 1967, we had opened for Cream a couple of times, and I remember Eric telling me that he liked the way I played. After that, I'm sure he saw me in concert once or twice with Hookfoot or Elton, and of course he would have heard me playing on the albums. But I hadn't seen him in nearly thirty years, and I hadn't been in the music business for sixteen years. Yet here he was announcing on national television that I was still the best guitar player in the world!

At least, that's what CBS News in Portland was telling me. They sent a camera crew to the church that night and did a story on me and my ministry. That's when I understood that God had created one more opportunity for getting His Word out to the world.

Over time, I began to realize that God wanted me to focus my efforts on this aspect of my ministry, leaving the administrative side to those with stronger gifts in those areas. In January of 2000, under the direction of the Lord, I left the headquarters office to establish my own itinerant ministry, New World Music Ministries Inc., which was designed to serve the Body of Christ with anointed music, worship, and preaching leading to a fresh encounter with Jesus. I became an evangelist, conference speaker, church consultant, and preacher whose Fender Strat was always by his side.

My wife Lydia was totally supportive of my decision to establish my own ministry. She's a substitute schoolteacher, but she volunteered to oversee the finances of New World Music Ministries, serving as the corporation CFO. We are both dedicated to spreading the Good News of the Gospel, and I certainly would not have been able to do what I've done without her love and support.

I had some amazing experiences as the head

of New World Music Ministries. For example, from 1999 to 2005, I had the privilege of playing with the Luis Pulau Praise Band at some of his events. Luis is a wonderful evangelist who at that time was holding incredible festivals drawing many thousands of people, similar in scope to the Billy Graham crusades. In fact, Luis had long been associated with Billy Graham and was considered by many to be his successor. Originally from Argentina, Luis could preach equally fluently in English or Spanish. The highlight of my time with him was playing at an enormous festival at Myrtle Beach, South Carolina to a crowd of 300,000 people. It has been reported that this was the largest single evangelical gathering in America since the Great Awakening! What a thrill it was when Luis gave an invitation at the end of his message and 20,000 people raised their hands signifying that they were opening their hearts to Jesus.

In 2006, I experienced another highlight as part of the worship team for the 100th anniversary of the Azusa Street Revival in Los Angeles. It had been a century since the outpouring of the Holy Spirit that birthed many Pentecostal and Charismatic movements around the world, including the Assemblies of God and the International Church of the Foursquare Gospel. The Los Angeles Convention Center was packed for a weeklong celebration, with many thousands of people and church leaders from around the world in attendance. I distinctly remember playing my guitar in the midst of a powerful time of worship during this event, and realizing that God had known and purposed before I was born that I would be there doing what I love to do for Him! In my mind as a musician who understands where the gift comes from, it just doesn't get any better.

But the most amazing experience of all has to be when I sing over people and see God heal them. For example, one time I was playing and preaching in a small rural church in Tennessee when the Lord led me to call a lady out of the congregation.

"You've got emphysema, don't you?" I said.

"Yes, I do," she replied. So I played guitar and sang over her while some of the others laid hands on her. After a while, she fell to the floor and began weeping and breathing heavily. The next night she came back and said she'd had the best night's sleep she'd ever had. During the worship service that night, she was dancing.

I know some of you are rolling your eyes and going, "Yeah, right." Was this women permanently cured, or was it just some psychosomatic, emotional reaction that would soon fade? I don't know, but I do know that it helped her and gave her hope.

The idea of healing through faith is an easy target for ridicule in our society, and there's no doubt it has attracted its share of charlatans. On the other hand, if you believe in an omnipotent God, it's not hard to believe that He might choose to heal people through faith. The Bible makes it clear that Jesus Christ healed people during His earthly ministry, and the book of Acts says that the disciples did so after His resurrection. It's obvious that God has the power to heal people through the Holy Spirit if He so chooses. The only question is whether He continues to heal people in today's world. For those who sneer at the idea, I only have one thing to say: I may not be able to prove that God still heals people, but you can't prove that He doesn't!

And before you dismiss the idea of healing by faith, remember that for most of us, the ailments that need healing are not physical, but spiritual, emotional, and behavioral. One time in New York, I was playing piano during a worship service and giving my testimony about being delivered from my drug habit. Some of the members of the church asked me to sing over a man they had been ministering to for a long-term heroin addiction. This guy was a mess—thin and filthy. I sang over him, and the Lord delivered him of his addiction then and there, just as He had done for me years before. The next night, a lady came up to me and thanked me for delivering her husband. I turned to see a man standing with his four children, and I didn't recognize him. It turned out that it was the heroin addict, but he literally looked like a new man. He had not only cleaned up, he looked so healthy that it was hard to believe he had ever been an addict.

If God has the power to heal this man and end his drug addiction just as He did mine, why can't He just as easily take away the pain of someone's arthritis? If He can take away the burden of guilt from an abusive alcoholic like my father, why can't he help an asthmatic to breathe easier? Each of us is free to believe or reject such claims—as for myself, I never cease to be amazed at the power of God's supernatural intervention.

In 2004, in addition to my work with New World Music Ministries, I became an adjunct faculty member in the music department of Life Pacific College in San Dimas, California. Established in the early 1920s, Life Pacific College is a Christian college affiliated with the Foursquare Church. I continued to teach there until 2009 and really enjoyed the experience. After a bit of a break, I became a part-time music teacher in the Cornel School of Contemporary Music at Shepherd University in Los Angeles, another Christian college.

In 2008, I was asked to put together a band to play at a conference at Viola University. I brought in my old friend Pee Wee Hill to play bass, then added Doug Mathews on drums and Charles Williams on keyboards. We called ourselves The Faculty because three of us were on faculty at Life Pacific College at the time. We enjoyed the gig so much that we're still together, playing clubs as well as churches. We primarily play instrumental jazz, but most of the titles are inspired by biblical verses or other spiritual writings or concepts, and between numbers I'll often talk briefly about those inspirations. Sometimes we do jazz arrangements of gospel songs. It gives me the opportunity to take light into dark places. It's like undercover evangelism, if you will, but the musicianship is solid, and we've never had anyone complain.

In 2014, Tim Clark became the new senior pastor at The Church on the Way in Los Angeles, where my spiritual journey began. I had known Tim since he was about 25, when he was starting out in ministry as a youth pastor at a Foursquare church. I became one of his mentors and we became friends, meeting at Starbucks once a month to discuss life and work. When I helped plant a Foursquare church on the campus of Liberty University, we brought him in as the senior pastor there. He went on to serve as a district supervisor for the denomination. Then one day, during our regular meeting at Starbucks, he told me about his new position at The Church on the Way. I was very pleased for my young friend and congratulated him heartily. Then he looked at me and said, "Caleb, I'd really like you to come on board with me. I really need your voice over there." So, just like that, I became the Elder of Worship, a part-time job with an office but no administrative duties. I play with the praise band, plan and lead worship services, and help keep the worship team on track both spiritually and logistically. In addition, as always, I help mentor the youth of the church.

With all this going on at home, I realized it was time to come back off the road. After all, I had been travelling regularly for almost twenty years, first for Foursquare and then for my own ministry. So I closed down New World Music Ministries and officially considered myself semi-retired, although I seem to be as busy as ever. In fact, I still travel occasionally to play and speak at churches and conferences, so how much has really changed I'm not sure.

About the same time, another chapter of my life seemed to close, at least symbolically.

After I left the music business in the early 1980s, I didn't see my friend and bandmate Roger Pope for almost twenty years. In 1999, during the same trip on which I visited with my father for the last time, the members of Hookfoot held an informal reunion in Southampton, England, at the home of Roger and his life partner Sue Tresidder. We vowed not to let so much time go by again, so ten years later we reconvened at Roger and Sue's to share a laugh and tell again the same old stories we already knew so well. I'm glad we did, because in early 2013 we received word that Roger had been diagnosed with cancer. Then we were told it was a particularly aggressive type of cancer and that our old friend had only six months to live. Sue kept us posted by Facebook, but unfortunately the reports did not improve.

One nice moment came when Roger and Sue were married there in his hospital room. The way it happened was kind of funny. They had been talking about getting married the following spring, when Roger was feeling better. When it became apparent that wasn't going to happen, Roger told Sue his only regret was that they had not had time to get married. Well, a nurse overheard him and said "We can arrange that!" Three hours later they were married there in his hospital room, and the long-suffering and ever-supportive Sue Tressider became Mrs. Sue Pope.

In early September, Sue let me know that Roger was not long for this world. I called and had a long, last telephone conversation with my mate. At one point I found myself crying. I was supposed to be comforting Roger, but instead he started comforting me! In return, I began sharing Christ with him. Roger wasn't one for organized religion or putting labels on people, but he believed in an afterlife. There on the phone, he accepted Christ into his life and I prayed for him. Sue says that "After the phone call, Roger was quiet and asked me to give him a hug. We clung to each other for a long time, the reality sinking in."

On September 18, 2013, Roger passed away.

I wasn't able to make it to the funeral in England, but I sent a memorial tribute that someone read during the service:

> Please accept my sincere apologies for not being able to be there with you all for such a time as this, but know that I am there with you in spirit as we honor the memory of our dear friend.
>
> I first met Roger Pope in 1965 on the set of ITV's *Ready Steady Go!*, when I was 16 years old and he was playing drums for The Soul Agents, backing the legendary blues guitarist Buddy Guy. When they started playing, Roger was driving the band with a very solid blues shuffle groove that was uncommon among English drummers in those days, and it caught my attention real quick. After the show, as he was packing up his kit, I went over and introduced myself and told him how much I enjoyed his playing.

About six months later, at the ripe old age of 17, I was working as a studio engineer at Dick James Music. One day, to my surprise, The Soul Agents showed up with their manager to audition for the label. I had the pleasure of recording them, and Roger remembered meeting me back at the TV show. From that point on, we struck up a friendship based on our common interest in music, primarily blues and jazz. Little did we know at the time that it would be a friendship that would last all these years, taking us on an incredible journey that included making some music that would become part of the musical history of the 20th century!

I'll never forget the day when he called me on the phone from Andover after we had recorded Lady Samantha, an early single for Elton John. He was insistent that we form a band together. I was living in London at the time and in his excitement he made a statement I have never forgotten: "Come on man, let's form a band. You tell me when and where and I'll get ten endorsements [speeding tickets] comin' up there!"

I spoke to him a few months ago and told him I was planning to come over to the UK soon and would love to see him. Would you believe after all these years (45 to be exact) he says to me, "Let me know where you'll be and I'll get ten endorsements!" Needless to say we had a good laugh on that one!

As I sit here writing these words, my mind is flooded with amazing memories of incredible recording sessions, rehearsals and gigs, and stadium concerts with Hookfoot, Elton John, Hall & Oates, and a great little band we had in Los Angeles in the early '80s called The Troops. I find it incredible to think that I will not see my "Chavvy" (Roger's favorite slang term for "friend") anymore in this world!

Sue, I want to thank you for your devotion and care of my friend, especially during the rough spots! He would not have made it this far without you. I'm so sorry I wasn't able to make it for the wedding. If I had known that was going to happen, I would have gotten ten endorsements myself!

Roger and I were big Jimi Hendrix fans and we loved a lyric in his song "Voodoo Chile" that says, "If I don't meet ya no more in this world, I'll meet ya in the next one. Don't be late!" Being a man of Christian faith, I am strengthened by the joy of having the privilege of praying with Roger in the hospital before he left us. I will never forget his response of love and thankfulness for that prayer, therefore I remain fully confident that he made it safely to the other side and that he will reserve a spot for me in the band when I get there!

Chapter Twelve

The Glamorous Life

When I was on the road as a rock guitarist, I was picked up by limousines and driven to cookie-cutter hotels where I would hang out with people I didn't know and would probably never see again. When I went out on the road for God, I was picked up at the airport by church pastors or elders who invited me into their homes and became my friends. Instead of waiting in perpetual boredom for the show to start or for the bus to leave for the next town, I met with various staff members to discuss ways to improve their worship services. Instead of staying up all night partying and taking drugs, a group of us would go to the local Denny's after the worship service, enjoy blossoming friendships over a late dinner, and retire to a restful sleep to start fresh the next day.

Most importantly, instead of staying on the road six months at a time as I had in the old days (and as my father had before me), my travel schedule was now carefully coordinated to the needs of my family. I made sure not to miss any important events in my children's lives ("important" being defined by what was important to them), and I made it a point not to stay gone more than several days at a time, even if it meant backtracking before going on to the next church.

Does it sound like I'm just getting old and slowing down? Maybe I am. But let me tell you what I'm not: I'm not ashamed of anything I do.

I'm not worried about anything. I'm not lonely. I don't feel lost. I don't wonder what life is all about. I don't sneak around hoping that I won't get caught. I never feel wiped out or "out of it." I don't worry about getting arrested or getting a disease. I don't ever wonder if anybody cares about me. And I don't end up looking in the mirror and thinking, "There's got to be more to it than this."

I may not have the glamour of the past, but I do have friends, and a loving family, and a steady income, and peace and happiness and contentment. I may not be living the glamorous life, but I am living the abundant life, just as the Bible promises. Maybe not financially, but in all the ways that really matter in life.

Where I used to play raucous rock & roll to

kids who were lost and rebellious, now I play songs of hope to teenagers who are searching their way to adulthood. After I play and speak, we discuss their very real concerns about life. Inevitably, I end up staying afterward to talk individually with some of the young people struggling with especially difficult circumstances. Where before I exploited the angst of teenagers to sell records, now I actually help them work through their problems and find a way out of the darkness with the light of Jesus Christ as their guide.

You may think that getting a gold record is glamorous, but let me tell you, it will never make you feel as good as when a hurting young person hugs you with tears in his or her eyes because you've shown them love they've never gotten at home. All the gold records in the world won't give you the lump in your throat you'll get when you receive a handwritten note—complete with misspellings and poor grammar—from a child you spoke to six months before who has decided to stay in school and who has found a family in the Body of Christ.

People often ask me, "Don't you miss all that fame and fortune? Don't you miss playing for 50,000 people at Dodger Stadium? Don't you miss those gold and platinum albums?"

I say, "You know, I used to own twelve guitars, but then I realized something. I realized I can only play one at a time. In the same way, I've realized that I can only serve one master. I can serve rock & roll, or I can serve God. I can focus my attention on getting rich and famous, or I can focus it on my family. I can put all my time and energy into selling more records than the next guy, or I can put it into caring for my children, building my church, being involved in my neighborhood, helping those less fortunate, and generally loving others."

You can have the glamorous life, or you can have the abundant life described in the Bible, but it's almost impossible to have both. As my testimony has demonstrated, the glamorous life is transitory, ready to evaporate like a shadow at any moment. And let me tell you the dirty little secret about the glamorous life: It ain't so glamorous!

Sitting in the audience at a concert, you see multi-colored lights and costumes and theatrics, and it provides you with an exciting break from your daily routine. But do you know what lies behind those speakers and those curtains? Nothing but concrete floors with cables running across them. Cinder-block walls and bare dressing rooms. Scaffolding and stacks of metal folding chairs and boxes and crates. Dark and cold corridors leading you out to the rented limousine, which whisks you back to the rented hotel room, where you have nothing to do but hang out with drunk and stoned people whose conversation is always shallow and whose motives are always suspect.

It's the hotel rooms that eat a hole in your soul. You arrive in a city the day before a concert, having just spent ten hours on a bus, or five hours getting to an airport, waiting to board your flight, flying, getting your luggage, and getting to your hotel. Now you have nothing to do but sit around while the roadies unload and set up the stage equipment. Finally, anywhere from 24 to 72 hours after the last show, you go on stage and spend three glorious hours basking in the spotlight. Then the wait starts all over again.

When you come off the stage after a three-hour concert, your adrenaline is pumping. It's almost midnight, but you're not going to be going to sleep anytime soon. You can't go out to the clubs, because you'll be mobbed if the word gets out, and even if you're not, it will just be a matter of time before some drunk tough guy decides he's got something to prove by picking on the famous guys. But you don't need the clubs, because you've got groupies and drugs right there in the hotel. You party all night with people who don't have anything better to do with their lives than follow bands around, then fall into bed exhausted. You wake up tired and hung over and start the process all over again.

Now try living like that six months in a row, then taking a month off, then doing it for another six months. It's no wonder musicians get hooked on drugs—it's the only way to make it through the immense slabs of boredom punctuated by the two or three hours of the shows.

Is the glamorous life of show business really glamorous? Was it glamorous when Jimi Hendrix and Janis Joplin and Elvis Presley and Michael Jackson and Prince all died young from drug abuse?

Was it glamorous the night that Motley Crue bassist Nikki Sixx had to have a shot of adrenaline straight to the heart in order to survive? Was it glamorous when George Michael was caught propositioning a male police officer in a public restroom, or when he sustained a brain injury when he fell out of his own moving car on the motorway? Was is glamorous when David Crosby spent nine months in jail for drug charges, or when he later collapsed with Hepatitis C and liver failure that required a transplant in order to save his life? (Crosby himself said, "I took it as far as I could take it without killing myself.")

What about when funk singer Rick James went to prison for kidnapping and torturing a woman? Or when rapper Tupac Shakur was gunned down on the streets of Las Vegas at the age of twenty-five? Or when R&B singer R. Kelly was indicted in 2002 on charges of child pornography, charges stemming from a videotape that allegedly showed him having sex with an underage girl?

In the 1960s, Syd Barrett, a founding member of Pink Floyd, and Brian Jones, a founding member of The Rolling Stones, were kicked out of their bands because of bizarre and irresponsible behavior brought on by drug abuse. In the 1970s, Sid Vicious of the Sex Pistols apparently murdered his girlfriend while high, then died six months later of a drug overdose that was almost certainly intentional. In 1980, Ben Scott, lead singer of AC/DC, died of alcohol abuse at the age of thirty-three. (After a night of drinking, Scott passed out in his car and choked to death on his own vomit.) In 1991, Def Leppard guitarist Steve Clark died of alcohol-related respiratory failure at the age of thirty. In 1994, at the age of twenty-seven, Kurt Cobain of the grunge band Nirvana shot himself. In 1997, Michael Huntchence, lead singer of INXS, committed suicide in a hotel room by hanging himself with his belt. (His wife, Paula Yates, died of an accidental drug overdose three years later.) In 2001, Stuart Adamson, lead singer of the rock band Big Country, committed suicide by hanging himself in a Honolulu hotel room. In 2002, Layne Staley, lead singer of Alice in Chains, was found dead of a drug overdose.

Earlier I mentioned that I worked with Mick Jagger while he was dating Marianne Faithfull.

Marianne had a string of hits in the mid-1960s, the most famous being "As Tears Go By." She later became a heroin addict, and at one point she ended up living in an abandoned building with other junkies. Glamorous, indeed.

The same is true of Hollywood. Was it glamorous when John Belushi died of a drug overdose in a hotel room, or when River Phoenix did so on the sidewalk outside an L.A. nightclub? What about when George Reeves, television's original Superman, killed himself? Or when Bob Crane, Hogan of *Hogan's Heroes*, was found beaten to death in his apartment, which was filled with hundreds of pornographic videos, some purchased and some homemade?

Was it glamorous when comic actor Pee

Wee Herman was caught masturbating in an adult theater, when Rob Lowe was caught videotaping himself having sex with an underage girl, or when *Chinatown* director Roman Polanski was charged with statutory rape for having sex with a thirteen-year-old girl and had to flee the country to avoid prosecution? Was it glamorous when actor Hugh Grant cheated on his live-in girlfriend Elizabeth Hurley by purchasing sex from a Hollywood streetwalker, or when Eddie Murphy was caught with a male transvestite prostitute?

The list goes on and on. Brett Butler's hit television show *Grace Under Fire* ended because she had to go into rehab for a second time. Adam Rich, one of the children on *Eight is Enough*, was arrested in 1991 for breaking into a pharmacy to steal drugs, then rearrested almost immediately after his release. Lisa Robin Kelly, the snotty sister on *That '70s Show*, died of a drug overdose at forty-three. Robert Downey Jr.'s drug arrests became so tedious he jokingly said that drugs and alcohol make him "break out in handcuffs." By the grace of God he overcame his addictions and rebounded in his career, but we all know he is the exception to the rule.

And it's not just show biz where the sinful nature of man makes itself obvious. It's true of every group we tend to think of as glamorous—sports, politics, the very rich. Scratch just below the surface and you'll find the stench of sin every time.

The examples I've listed above are just a tiny fraction of the scandals and tribulations and tragedies of those living the "glamorous life" that have made the headlines. And for every one that makes the headlines, there are dozens, if not hundreds, of lives damaged and destroyed that never make it into the paper. Drugs, drinking, and infidelity run rampant through these areas of society. Money, fame, and power are exciting intoxicants to some people, but the fun that is to be had by indulging oneself leads inevitably to the hangover of the morning after—assuming you live until morning.

Some of you are sitting there thinking, "Now, wait a minute, Caleb. Sure, people in show biz do some things wrong, but so does everyone else. These people are no different from society as a whole." You're right, and that's just my point.

These people are no better than anyone else, and they are faced with temptations that would make most people go astray. And yet they are the people providing the music our children listen to, producing the movies and television shows our children watch, and serving as the role models that our children strive to emulate.

Before you take such people as your idols and role models, ask yourself this: What kind of person is so intoxicated by money, fame, and power that they would focus their entire lives on acquiring those things? Are these healthy, stable people? I loved the money and fame that came with being a rock star, but years later I discovered that these things meant something to me only because I didn't have what I really wanted—the love and respect of my father. Once I learned to accept myself as I was and to forgive others, I immediately lost all interest in the life that I knew was anything but glamorous.

Elton was motivated by similar factors in his early career. You'll recall that one reason Elton and I became friends as teenagers was that we both had absentee fathers who never showed us love or attention. Elton's father was overly strict with him, and Elton has said in interviews that his wild stage costumes were his way of cutting loose in a way he wasn't allowed to as a child. Always shy with people one-on-one, Elton has often stated that he feels most comfortable on stage behind his piano. Elton is immensely talented, and I'm not suggesting for a moment that he doesn't deserve his fame and fortune. But I think even he realizes that his powerful ambition to "make it" was originally fueled largely by a search for validation. I know mine was.

That's a common story among ambitious people, especially those who seek success in the public arena. Marilyn Monroe, for example, is still considered by many to be the epitome of glamour, but any study of her life will reveal a deeply insecure, troubled young lady who craved approval because she never got it at home. Raped as a teenager and never shown the love she needed, she clung to anything and anyone that would make her feel valuable as a person. The song "Candle in the Wind," Elton and Bernie's classic ode to Marilyn, captures this situation perfectly. Marilyn used Hollywood to fulfill her own desperate needs, and

Hollywood took advantage of her needs in order to exploit her to its own ends.

Many comedians have admitted in interviews that they used comedy in their childhoods as a way of gaining approval from their parents, or to win friends at school, or to cover up their various sadnesses. Many others have acknowledged the obvious—they joke around to cover up deep-seated insecurities. They are afraid to be serious because they are afraid that no one will take them seriously, especially members of the opposite sex. The cliché of the "crying clown" could be applied to virtually any area of public endeavor.

Do you dream of playing guitar in front of 50,000 people at Dodger Stadium? If so, I would encourage you to ask yourself why the cheers of people you don't know would make you happy. What is missing in your emotional life that you can only feel validated by the adulation of throngs of strangers? Perhaps instead of asking how you can get rich and famous, or how you can win the best-looking girl or guy, or how you can climb to the top of the social ladder in your school or community, perhaps you should instead be asking why you aren't happy with yourself as you are. Because if you aren't happy with yourself, I can tell you from my own experience that none of those other things will make you happy.

If playing for 50,000 people at Dodger Stadium is what brings you joy, then more power to you. But as someone who has done it, I can safely say that you don't know what real joy is yet. Experiencing true joy requires the ability to forget about your worries, to face others openly and unashamed, to have no hidden agenda, no ambition, no self-interest, no pride. You can do this only if you have found someone else to take all your problems and to take care of your future. The only one who can truly do that for you is Jesus Christ.

There is an alternative to the glamorous life that the world dangles in front of you, and that is the abundant life promised to us in the Bible. Where the glamorous life is as transparent and elusive as the end of a rainbow, the abundant life offered by God is stable, grounded, centered, and, best of all, it will last throughout eternity! Once you experience the joy that comes from turning your life over to

Jesus Christ, all the joys of our material and transient world put together won't impress you. In the last chapter, I'm going to explain how you can claim this joy for yourself.

Chapter Thirteen

The Rebellious Heart

Well, there's no getting around it. Here I am, a reformed rock & roll guitarist giving my testimony as a born-again Christian, while the rock star with whom I am most closely associated is, as he puts it, the most famous homosexual in the world. Elton John is not only the most famous celebrity in the world who is known to be gay; he is also famous for *being* gay. He is quite open about his sexual preference, and he is an outspoken supporter of gay rights. While his work in the fight against AIDS in the gay community has drawn widespread praise, his use of gay-themed vulgarity in interviews and his tendency to "camp it up" has been seen as less than tasteful. In the spring of 2000, for example, he drew criticism even from some in the gay community when he had a group of young men dressed as Boy Scouts do a strip tease during one of his shows.

Where does all this leave me? Elton John is not only my friend, he is virtually my oldest friend. He was my closest associate in the music business. And yet he openly, even blatantly, lives a lifestyle that conflicts with the teachings of the Christian religion that I not only embrace, but that I have been called to proclaim throughout the world.

How do I reconcile this dichotomy? Am I called on by my faith to publicly condemn my own friend, or can I, as the Bible teaches, truly learn to hate the sin but love the sinner? My answer may surprise you.

I'm not really sure when I first became aware of Elton's homosexuality, but it probably wasn't long after he became aware of it himself. When we met as teenagers, I know for a fact that he didn't think of himself as gay. You'll recall that he dated and even lived with a woman during the time we played with Long John Baldry, and Elton was around twenty years old at that time.

In my opinion, Long John Baldry had a lot to do with Elton either choosing or allowing himself to go in that direction. Baldry was a flaming homosexual whose campy posturing Elton soon adopted. Baldry called himself and others by feminine nicknames like "Ada" and "Shirley," a habit that Elton continues to this day. Baldry and

Reg became close, and while I don't think there was a sexual relationship there, I think Baldry was a definite influence. He was Elton's mentor.

In fact, we all respected Baldry, because he'd been in the business for a long time—he had done gigs with The Beatles at the Cavern Club before they were big. He was older than us, and he taught us a lot. But he was outrageous too. I remember him running up and down hotel corridors jokingly chasing little boys. To Elton, a young man desperately seeking a father figure, Baldry legitimized something that Elton may already have been feeling. Even Elton's own mum has publicly stated that she doesn't think he would have become gay had he not gone into the music business.

When Elton finally broke through in

America with the second album, I had already formed Hookfoot. Dick James had encouraged Elton to get a manager, and he chose John Reid, previously the British rep for Motown Records. When Elton first introduced me to Reid, I noticed that they were wearing sort of identical clothes and identical haircuts, and I remember thinking, "Okay, something's going on here." In an interview in *Rolling Stone*, Elton said that the first time he had sex was with Reid at the age of 23, but at that time we didn't realize they were lovers. They moved into an apartment together, but we all assumed they were just flatmates. His recent comments make it obvious that he was already into an alternative lifestyle that his straight friends knew nothing about.

In 1975, when I flew down to Arizona to discuss rejoining Elton, his homosexual lifestyle was more apparent. His entourage was made up mainly of people like John Reid, Tony King, and Ian Brown, all of whom we knew to be gay. And Billie Jean King had recently generated significant publicity when she admitted having a lesbian relationship. When we went on tour that year, the excesses of Elton's lifestyle became more and more obvious to those of us in the band. I remember, for example, the transvestite Divine showing up for a couple of concerts. As I said earlier, Elton had his own crowd that he would hang around with after the shows, separate from the rest of the band. Of course, all this was kept carefully under wraps until Elton blew the whistle on himself in the 1976

Rolling Stone interview.

Even then, however, Elton referred to himself as "bisexual," and I don't think he was using that term only to avoid the term "homosexual." I think he had not yet come to see himself as completely gay. In interviews, he still talked about how nice it would be to have a family and a house with the white picket fence. And in 1983, he actually married a wonderful woman named Renate Blauel, a marriage that lasted about four years.

Elton has publicly acknowledged that, in hindsight, he married Renate in a desperate attempt to bring some normalcy to his life. He thought she would save him from his demons. At the same time, everyone around them seems to agree that Elton really loved her, so the capacity to share romantic love with a female did exist in him. It was only after the failure of that marriage, toward the end of 1988, when Elton was forty-one years old, that he finally looked at himself as fully and permanently gay. By that time, of course, the whole world looked at him that way.

How did I react when I first began to learn these things about Elton? To be honest, I had no reaction. I wasn't shocked because I wasn't looking at it from a moral standpoint. I was far from being a Christian, and this was the '70s. As I've said, the slogan back then was, "If it feels good, do it." To me, it was all part of being in the music business. I didn't really have an opinion about it one way or the other.

Now, of course, being a Christian, I have

very definite views about homosexuality, and I could easily launch into a sermon about it. But that would be to miss the main point of Christianity.

Just what is the main point of Christianity? Let me put it this way: When God looks at Elton John, He may be concerned about Elton's homosexuality, but that is not what He is *primarily* concerned about. What God is *primarily* concerned about is the rebellious heart that keeps Elton separated from Him. And He sees that same rebellious heart in you and me, in heterosexuals as well as homosexuals, in men as well as women, in black as well as white, and in every country around the world.

God is not concerned primarily about our sexual habits or any of our other habits. He is primarily concerned about the state of our hearts, and it is the state of our hearts that creates our habits anyway. I myself spent the best part of two decades in almost daily drug abuse and adultery—was I any closer to God just because my illicit sexual activity was heterosexual instead of homosexual? Not according to the Bible. I was separated from God not by my sinful activities, but by the rebellious heart that led to those activities, that justified those activities, and that even celebrated those activities.

In an earlier chapter, I talked about Bernie Taupin's first wife, Maxine, living openly with another member of the band while we were recording the *Rock of the Westies* album in Colorado. You'll recall that my reaction was the same then as it was to Elton's homosexuality—"If it feels good, do it." Yet in God's eyes, that was every bit as sinful as homosexuality. In fact, the Bible states that all sins are equal in the eyes of God. That's a hard thing to comprehend until you realize that the problem is not the individual sinful action, but the rebellious state of heart that leads to those actions.

Did I have a rebellious state of heart before I found Jesus? Absolutely, and look where it got me. Does Elton have a rebellious heart? Anyone who has followed his career knows that he does. He is legendary for losing his temper when things don't go the way he wants them to. He has stormed out of recording sessions, video tapings, and show rehearsals. Even in his fifties he was still saying vulgar things just to shock people. And even he admits that, by the 1980s, he had gone a little too far with his attention-getting costumes.

What is Elton rebelling against? The same thing I was rebelling against—a father who left me feeling unloved and unlovable. That, I believe, is why Elton spoke out against Dick James with such anger after all the man had done for us. Dick James had been like a father to Elton, and Elton hated his father.

And God is supposed to be our heavenly Father. It's been said that a person's relationship with their biological father will set the pattern for their relationship with their heavenly father. Whether that is true for Elton is between him and God, but it certainly was true for me. The anger I had carried around my entire life wasn't healed until I knelt down, forgave my biological father, and turned my anger over to my heavenly Father. Letting go of that anger was the beginning of a healthy and loving relationship with both of them.

What about you? What is standing between you and God? Whatever it is, I encourage you to kneel down, forgive others, and turn your anger and guilt over to Him. You've got nothing to lose but your unhappiness.

Yes, there is a higher power in this universe, and it has a name. By calling on that name, praying in that name, repenting to that name, and relying on that name, you can find your burdens lightened and your life made whole. It's as simple as that.

You see, this book isn't about Elton John,

and it's not even really about me. This book is about you. It's about where you're going in life and where you stand with God. This book wasn't written to give me a chance to talk about myself; it was written as a warning to you about the emptiness of the rebellious life and the glory that God offers as an antidote to that emptiness.

As I said earlier, during my teenage years, music became my life. I later came to realize why. Music had become my life because I had nothing else in my life. I was using music as a substitute to fill the void left by my father's abuse and desertion. Lacking the love I so desperately wanted, I used music to ease the pain. It was, as the psychologist would say today, my "mood-altering" habit, something I used to distance myself from the pain of my reality. Of course, soon it wasn't enough, so I added drugs, then a sex addiction. And like all addictions, I found that I needed more and more to get me "high" and to keep me from having to acknowledge the harsh realities of my life.

The Bible has a word for such things. It calls them "idols." Anything that you have placed at the center of your life to the exclusion of loving God and loving your neighbor has become your idol, and it is a false idol that will lead you down an unfulfilling, if not destructive, path. One of the Ten Commandments says, "Thou shall have no other gods before me." Don't make the mistake of thinking that this refers only to the strange, multi-armed gods of other lands. We can make anything our god—music, drugs, sex, ambition, pride, money, work, play, other people. We often do this to shield ourselves from the harsh realities of life, but in doing so, we prevent ourselves from ever encountering the ultimate reality that is Jesus Christ our Lord.

Ironically, it is possible to use religious faith in precisely the same way, as a mood-altering agent that some people wrap around themselves like a fluffy blanket to keep out all the bad thoughts of the world. There are, unfortunately, those who are as addicted to their religion as I was to music and drugs. They find themselves always needing more; they can never be religious enough, until they are so consumed with the idea of being religious that they cannot reach anyone from inside their cocoon.

That wasn't the case with me. Religion for

me was never about escapism. In fact, it wasn't until I found Jesus Christ that I was able to face the pain in my life. With Jesus on my side, I had the strength to look at myself and others with all our imperfections and to face up to the evil that had invaded my life. Only when you admit that others have been bad to you can you begin to forgive them; only when you admit that you have been bad to others can you begin to seek their forgiveness. Rather than wrapping myself in a protective cloak of religiosity, I find myself instead reaching out to others more and more, letting God's light shine through me into the world.

What are your idols? What are you using to keep from facing up to and overcoming the barriers in your life? Chances are that by turning to false idols and trying to ignore the problem, you're really just making the problem worse.

So your parents don't love you—are those drugs making you feel any more loved? So you're not popular in school—are those freaky clothes and that go-to-hell attitude making you any more popular? So you feel inadequate around the opposite sex—is getting drunk and getting into fights getting you any dates? So you can't master your schoolwork—is skipping school going to solve that problem?

It's not just true with young people. Men become frustrated when they don't progress in their careers as they had hoped, so they start drinking or slacking off, behavior that is sure to stall their careers even further. Husbands and wives don't like the way their marriage is working out, so they grow sullen or snide, behavior guaranteed to end a marriage instead of rescuing it. Middle-aged men confronted with the loss of their youth may have an affair to prove something to themselves. They still lose their youth, and now they may lose their family, as well.

In every one of these cases, people try to hide the truth from themselves and others by acting as if they don't care, but pretending you don't care will never do anything but prolong the pain. The only way to solve any problem is to admit that you *do* care and that you *do* want to solve the problem or, if the problem is beyond your control, to learn how to live with it. This can be a difficult and dark road to travel if you do so alone, but your burden can be made lighter if you make the journey with Jesus Christ.

You must let your idols go. You must stand alone, naked before the universe, facing up to the reality that is your life. You must acknowledge that things are not as they should be, that *you* are not as you should be. You must admit to God that you have done wrong, and that you are not happy with your life the way it is. You must repent of your rebellious heart and ask Jesus to come into your heart and abide there. You must ask Jesus to take away your old life, your old self. You must ask to be born again as a new creature in the Lord.

You may be wondering how God does this; the answer is through trusting Jesus for who He is and what He has done. You may be wondering why

He does this; the answer is because He loves us. You may be wondering when He does this; the answer is anytime you choose to ask Him in all sincerity, because the Bible says, *"ask, and you shall receive"* (John 16:24).

For obvious reasons, my "life verse" from the Bible is Second Corinthians 5:17, which states that *"If anyone is in Christ, he is a new creation; old things have passed away; behold, all things have become new."* It never ceases to amaze me how thoroughly God has transformed my life, and if He can do it for me, He can do it for anyone. You can be made a new creature by accepting Christ into your heart.

At the time this is being written, incredible things are happening in this world, quantum leaps in technology. The DNA code has been cracked—I guess that means designer people are on the way. In a recent scientific experiment, the speed of light was broken! They say that within ten years, lasers may be used to effectively cure cancer, HIV, and Alzheimer's. As incredible and wonderful as these scientific breakthroughs are, none of them can deal with the sinful nature of mankind, which drives us to kill and enslave and mistreat one another in an infinite variety of ways. And if you think that human nature is progressing beyond all that, you just haven't been paying attention to the news.

If history has proven anything, it's that sin is the incurable condition of mankind. Incurable, that is, by man's own efforts. But there is one remedy that is foolproof—The cross of Christ! This was

God's cure for our sinful natures, His way of building a bridge to span the gap between Him and us. He sent His only Son to sacrifice His life for us, that we would not perish in our sin, but have eternal life with Him. You will never change human nature on a global level, but you can change *your* nature, by committing your life to Christ.

"Those who are planted in the house of the LORD shall flourish in the courts of our God," says Psalm 92:13-15. *"They shall still bear fruit in old age; they shall be fresh and flourishing, to declare that the LORD is upright; He is my rock, and there is no unrighteousness in Him."* It is amazing to me that God has allowed me to bear fruit into middle age, and it is my prayer that he allows me to continue to do so into old age.

Back in the 1960s, the members of my generation thought we were going to bring about a new world free from all the problems of the old world. As a musician, I saw myself as an instrument in this revolution. But my generation failed, and I failed my generation. I couldn't even be a good husband and father, much less a leader pointing the way to a better life. Yet here I am, decades later, and God has turned my earlier experiences into a beacon of hope for a new generation. It is incredible to me that God would use me as an agent of blessing to an emerging generation in this new millennium.

As I look to the future, I am reminded of the promise given to us in Jeremiah 29:11, which says, *"For I know the thoughts that I think toward you, says the Lord, thoughts of peace and not of evil, to give you a future and a hope."* May you find your hope and your future where I have found mine—in the loving arms of the Lord Jesus Christ.

Prayer of Salvation

If something in this book has influenced you and you want to know the God I know, I'm more than happy to share Him with you. In these perilous times, it is important that you develop a relationship with Him right now. To know that your "forever" with Him is assured, repeat this simple prayer:

Thank you, Jesus, that you have made yourself known to me. You are not just a person to read about or hear about, but you are real and living. I believe that you are the Son of God who suffered and died on the Cross so that my sins might be forgiven, and that you rose from the dead and ascended into heaven to appear before the Father for my sake. I open my heart to you, and I put my trust in you as my Savior and the Lord of my life. Fill me with the Holy Spirit and help me to understand the Bible, so that I might live a life that is pleasing to you. Thank you for your mercy, forgiveness, and the free gift of salvation. Thank you for my membership in the family of God, in Jesus' name. Amen.

About the Authors

Caleb Quaye was born in London on October 9, 1948, the son and grandson of famous jazz musicians. In 1964, at the age of 15, he began working in the British music industry as an errand boy on Denmark Street. There he became friends with another errand boy named Reginald Dwight, who would later experience unparalleled pop music success as Elton John. Caleb produced and played guitar on Elton's early demos and singles, was instrumental in helping Elton secure his first recording contract, and played on seven of his classic '70s albums. During the same period, Caleb's band, Hookfoot, released four albums through A&M Records. He later toured with Hall &

Oates during the peak of their success. From the late '60s to the early '80s, Caleb was a well-known studio musician, playing with some of the top acts of the day.

In the early '80s, Caleb found a personal relationship with Jesus Christ and left the music business to enter the ministry. He served as national Director of Worship & Music for the International Church of the Foursquare Gospel for five years before establishing New World Music Ministries in 2000. Today, Caleb travels the world speaking and playing music to churches and to whoever will listen! He is currently serving on the worship team at NewLife a Fourquare church in Pomona California.

Dale A. Berryhill is a Christian author with four other books to his credit. In addition, he has written and produced multiple books and videos documenting corporate histories and personal or family memoirs through his award-winning marketing communications firm, Berryhill Communications Inc. (www.BerryhillCommunications.com). For ten years beginning in 1995, he was a regular contributor to *East End Lights* magazine, a high-quality Elton John fanzine, for which he interviewed many of Elton's past and present band members, lyricists, producers, album cover designers, record company executives, and costume designers. He was featured on the BBC for his research in England on places that inspired some of the early Elton John songs, as well as spots related to the lives and careers of Elton and his lyricist Bernie Taupin.

Caleb Quaye

Partial Discography:

For Elton John

- *The Dick James Demos* (1967-1969 DJM, not officially released)
    - lead guitar, production
- "I've Been Loving You" b/w "Here's to the Next Time" (1968 Philips)
    - lead guitar, production
- "Lady Samantha" b/w "All Across the Havens (1969 Philips)
    - lead guitar
- "It's Me That You Need" b/w "Just Like Strange Rain" (1969 DJM)
    - lead guitar
- *Empty Sky* (1969 DJM)
    - electric guitar, acoustic guitar, conga drums
- *Elton John* (1970 DJM)
    - lead guitar (tracks 3–5), additional guitars (track 9)
- *Tumbleweed Connection* (1970 DJM)
    - lead guitar, acoustic guitar, 12-string

- *Friends* (1971 Paramount) (movie soundtrack)
    - guitars
- *Madman Across The Water* (1971 DJM)
    - electric guitar (tracks 1–3), acoustic guitar (track 6)
- *Rock of the Westies* (1975 DJM)
    - acoustic guitar, electric guitar, rhythm guitar, backing vocals
- *Blue Moves* (1976 Rocket)
    - acoustic guitar, electric guitar, 12-string guitar, composer (track 1), co-composer (tracks 5, 11, 12)

With Hookfoot

Lead guitar, songwriting, lead vocals, backing vocals

- *Hookfoot* (1971 DJM/A&M)
- *Good Times A' Comin'* (1972 DJM/A&M)
- *Communication* (1973 DJM/A&M)
- *Roaring* (A&M 1974 DJM/A&M
- *Hookfoot Live in Memphis* (1974 DJM/A&M) (live)
- *Headlines* (1975 DJM) (compilation)

For Other Artists

Caleb played electric guitar on all projects unless otherwise noted. He did not necessarily play on all tracks of albums listed. If no project is listed, it is because session musicians do not always know when or where their work will appear.

- **The Beatles** – Christmas Fan Club single (1966 Parlophone) (sound engineer only, George Martin producing)
- **The Troggs**
    - *From Nowhere* (1966 Fontana)
    - "With A Girl Like You" (1966 Fontana)
    - *Trogglodynamite* (1967 Page One)
    - *Cellophane* (including the single "Love is All Around") (1967 Page One)
- **PP Arnold** – *First Lady Of Immediate* (1967 Immediate)
- **Mike McGear** – *McGough & McGear* (1968 Real Gone) (sound engineer only, Paul McCartney producing)
- **The Bread & Beer Band**
    - *The Bread & Beer Band* (1969 independent)
    - "Dick Barton Theme (The Devil's

Gallop)" (1969 Decca)
  - "Breakdown Blues" (1969 Decca) (also co-composer)
- **Long John Baldry** - *It Ain't Easy* (1971 Warner) (also organ)
- **Ralph McTell** – *Your Well Meaning Brought Me Here* (1971 Famous)
- **Bernie Taupin** – *Taupin* (1971 DJM) (piano, acoustic guitar, organ)
- **Nigel Olsson** *Nigel Olsson's Drum Orchestra and Chorus* (1971 DJM)
- **Tony Hazzard** – *Loudwater House* (1971 Bronze)
- **Al Kooper** – *New York City (You're a Woman)* (1971 Columbia)
- **Harry Nilsson** – *Nilsson Schmilsson* (including the single "Coconut") (1971 RCA)
- **Roger Cook** – *Meanwhile Back at the World* (1972 Regal Zonophone)
- **Mick Grabham** – *Mick the Lad* (1972 United Artists) (tracks 3 & 5, piano only)
- **Lou Reed** – *Lou Reed* (1972 RCA)
- **Pete Townshend** – *Who Came First* (1972 Track) (track 3, guitars, bass guitar, percussion)
- **Dick Heckstall Smith** – *A Story Ended* (1972 Bronze)
- **Yvonne Elliman** – *Food of Love* (1973 Decca)
- **Bobby Hatfield** – *Stay with Me* (1972

Warner Brothers)
- **Andrew Lloyd Webber** – (1973)
- **Willie Dixon** – (1974)
- **Billy Nicholls** – *Love Songs* (1974 GM)
- **Shawn Phillips** – *Furthermore* (1974 A&M)
- **The Who** – *Tommy* (1975 Polydor) (movie soundtrack)
- **Hall & Oates** –
    - *Along The Red Ledge* (1978 RCA)
    - *Livetime* (1978 RCA)
- **Liza Minnelli** – *Tropical Nights* (1977 Columbia)
- **Bruce Johnston** – *Going Public* (1977 Columbia)
- **Beach Boys** – *Keepin' The Summer Alive* (1980 Brother/Caribou/CBS)
- **Daryl Hall** – *Sacred songs* (1980 RCA)
- **Dusty Springfield** – *White Heat* (1980 Casablanca) (also synthesizer, bass, Wurlitzer, Mini Moog)
- **Eddie Henderson** – *Runnin' to Your Love* (1979 Capitol)
- **George Duke** – *Clarke/Duke Project* (1981 Epic/CBS)
- **David Foster** – (1981)
- **Jennifer Holliday** – *Feel My Soul* (1982 Geffen)
- **Phillip Bailey** – (1982)
- **Peter Criss** – *Let Me Rock You* (1982 Casablanca)
- **Brenda Russell** – *Two Eyes* (1983 Warner

Brothers)
- **Joan Baez** – *Recently* (1987 Gold Castle)
- **John Klemmer** – *Music* (1989 MCA)
- **And many more!**

Praise Music

- Caleb Quaye – *Light of the World* (2003) (Christmas album)
- Caleb Quaye – *The Work of His Hands* (2004 Potters New World Music)
- Caleb Quaye and The Faculty – *Out of the Blue* (2009)
- Caleb Quaye – *Devotions* (2013)

In 1968, Roger Pope (left) talked me into joining The Loot for a brief time. The band soon folded, but Roger, Dave Wright (to my right) and I formed Hookfoot, a more serious funk/fusion band. No more pop songs for us! Loot lead vocalist Dave Wright (front) moved on to other projects.

Jacket cover photo from the self-titled "Elton John" album in 1970.

A Quaye family photo in better times, circa 1956. From left to right: Terri, Tanya, Theresa (Mum), Caleb (8 years old), Cab (Dad)

Backstage at the California Ballroom in Dunstable, circa 1959. That's me holding the music for my Dad while he's rehearsing for the show. I used to watch him play guitar and dreamed of doing the same one day!

HOOKFOOT

Hookfoot's first album cover photo, taken at Roger's house in Andover, where we all lived for a while like hippies—eating, drinking, smoking pot, and becoming one of the tightest bands around.

HOOKFOOT

An early Hookfoot promo shot. We really loved the English Countryside, but perhaps we couldn't see the forest for the trees!

A Hookfoot press conference most probably in Atlanta, 1972, with Yours Truly pontificating about music and politics while trying to decipher a southern accent through all the hours of jet lag and road antics!

My marriage to my first wife, Patricia, at St. Paul's church in Finchley, England, February, 1972. The wedding took place in the middle of a tour in which my band, Hookfoot, was opening for Humble Pie. From left to right are: Bob Kulick (a guitarist who later played for Meatloaf), Dave Glover (bass player for Hookfoot), Derek Simms (Hookfoot roadie), Terry Carty (DJM Studio tape operator and tea maker), Roger Pope (Hookfoot drummer and best man), Phil Greenfield (Hookfoot's road manager, affectionately known as 'Phlop'), Elton John (cracking jokes in my ear), Ian Duck (Hookfoot's lead singer, hiding in the back), Jeff Titmus (DJM Studio engineer), and Gordon Sutherland (Chrysalis Record exec and friend).

Another Hookfoot press conference. As you can see, I was quite the hippie back then! From one point in the late 60's, I didn't cut my hair for ten years straight!

Back with Elton John for the 1975 UK tour called "Louder Than Concorde But Not Quite As Pretty" tour. Judging by the hat Elton is wearing, I would say this was taken in Edinburgh, Scotland. From left to right: guitarist Davey Johnstone, bassist Kenny Paserelli, Elton John, drummer Roger Pope, and yours truly.

Wembly Stadium, 1975. My first gig after rejoining Elton John. It was a long way from our days as teenage tea boys on Denmark Street, and it sure felt good to play a packed house. This photo was taken by Roger Pope from behind his drum kit in the middle of a song!

Fun times on the chartered jet with "Captain Fantastic" during the "Rock of the Westies" tour in 1975. Someone gave Elton a pair of roller skates, which he promptly put on and skated around the plane, much to everyone's delight. From left to right: Davey Johnstone, me, Elton, and Ken, one of the backup singers.

Album jacket cover photo from "Rock of the Westies" in 1975. That's me, second from left, complete with 'stash' pouch!

Kickin' it at Madison Square Garden in 1976. We were the first band ever to sell out the Garden for seven straight days. From left to right: Davey, Kenny, Elton, me, and the famous transvestite Divine.

We were doing four hour shows, and life was getting a little too crazy even for me. While we were in New York, Elton granted an interview with Rolling Stone magazine in which he acknowledged himself to be bisexual. At the end of the tour, he dissolved the band and went into the first of several "retirements" he has announced throughout his career.

With my wife Lydia on our wedding day, April 7, 1984 (Thank you Jesus!)

The Quaye family today: Caleb, Lydia & daughter Stephanie!

Printed in Great Britain
by Amazon